THE NON-LAWYERS LIVING TRUST KIT

2nd Edition

Special Book Edition
With Removeable Forms

By Kermit Burton

Alpha Publications Of America, Inc.
P.O. Box 12488 • Tucson, AZ 85732-2488
1-800-528-3494

Published by:
ALPHA PUBLICATIONS OF AMERICA, INC.
P.O. Box 12488
Tucson, Arizona 85732-2488

ISBN 0-937434-337

Check List Of The Removable
LIVING TRUST FORMS
Included In This Book

FORM	DESCRIPTION
AT-101-1	Declaration of Trust, Page 1 (Each Beneficiary Equally Sharing the Trust Property)
AT-101-2	Declaration of Trust, Page 1 (Each Beneficiary receiving a Fixed Percentage of the Trust Property)
AT-101-3	Declaration of Trust, Page 1 (Each Beneficiary receiving Specific Trust Property)
AT-102-1	Declaration of Trust, Page 2 (Trust Clause No. 2, The Trust Property)
AT-102-2	Declaration of Trust, Page 2 (Trust Clause No. 2, The Trust Property with numerical listing of property)
AT-103	Declaration of Trust, Page 3 (Trust Clauses No. 3 through 8)
AT-104	Declaration of Trust, Page 4 (Trust Clauses No. 9 through 14)
AT-105	Declaration of Trust, Page 5 (Trust Clauses No. 15 through 18 and the Notary Acknowledgment)
AT-200a-b	Deed of Realty To Trust, Pages 1 and 2
AT-201a-b	Quit Claim Deed To Trust, Pages 1 and 2
AT-202	Financial Account Transfer To Trust
AT-203	Securities Transfer To Trust
AT-204a-b	Assignment of Secured Realty Contract To Trust, Pages 1 and 2
AT-205a-b	Chattel Transfer To Trust, Pages 1 and 2
AT-206	Assignment of Non-Realty Contract To Trust
AT-207a-b	Business Interest Transfer To Trust, Pages 1 and 2
AT-300	Notice of Trust
AT-400a-b	A simple Pour-Over Last Will and Testament, Pages 1 and 2
AT-500	Disclaimer by Spouse
AT-600	Amendment To Trust Enlarging Powers Of Trustee(s)
AT-601a-b	Amendment to Trust Limiting Distribution of Assets to a Beneficiary, Pages 1 and 2
AT-700	Affidavit Of Successor Trustee's Authority To Administer Trust
AT-701	Medical Certification
AT-702	Affidavit Terminating Successor Trustee's Authority To Administer Trust
AT-900	Trust Activity Recording Log

The Forms described above, together with the included text material, constitute the whole of this Non-Lawyers Living Trust Kit. Therefore, all of the text material is directed toward purchaser's knowledgeable use of both the text material and the forms. However, neither the author nor the publisher intends to offer the information herein contained as legal advice, which can only be offered by an Attorney licensed to practice law in your state. And while all of the herein information is believed and thought to be accurate, neither the author nor the publisher assumes any liability in connection with the use of this information, and the application of the forms.

Affordable Legal Services For The Non-Lawyer . . . . .

by Alpha Publications of America, Inc.

Authored by Kermit Burton

The All New Perfect Bound Book Editions of The Non-Lawyer Legal Kits

- ☐ Each book is a complete **do-it-yourself** Legal Kit with **easy-to-remove** Legal Forms.
- ☐ Each book includes: **easy to understand text** material written especially for the Non Lawyer; **step-by-step instructions** that simplify the correct preparation of each Form; and fully **prepared examples** of each included Form.
- ☐ Each book includes **predrafted Legal Forms** which are applicable to the Laws of all States.
- ☐ Each book provides a **Toll Free 800 Number**.

The Retail Price and ISBN Number of each Book is as follows:

Book	ISBN	Price
A-B TRUST	0-937434-469	$18.95
BANKRUPTCY	0-937434-299	27.95
CHAPTER 13	0-937434-302	27.95
CORPORATION	0-937434-310	26.95
DIVORCE	0-937434-108 (California)	21.95
HOME SALES	0-937434-329	14.95
LIVING TRUST	0-937434-337	14.95
LIVING WILL	0-937434-345	16.95
NON-PROFIT CORP.	0-937434-353	29.95
PARTNERSHIP	0-937434-361	19.95
PRE-MARRIAGE	0-937434-37X	14.95
WILL	0-937434-388	14.95

ALPHA PUBLICATIONS OF AMERICA, INC.
4500 East Speedway, Suite 31
Tucson, AZ 85712-5325

(602) 795-7100 Anywhere 1-800-528-3494 Fax 1-800-770-4329

Table Of Contents

Table of Contents, Cont'd

Introduction

This **Non-Lawyers Living Trust Kit** provides to the non-lawyer, a low cost, simple and efficient way to protect the value of his or her estate from the high cost and potential abuses of the probate system.

The laws regarding Living Trust are few and simple, in fact, so simple that it causes most lawyers to disavow any knowledge of Living Trust when queried by their clients, which shows a lack of concern and caring for the needs of the community as a whole.

This is not at all surprising since Living Trusts do not command high legal fees as does the probating of a Will. Remember, when a Last Will and Testament is prepared by a Lawyer, the cost of this preparation is not cheap, and when the person passes, then there are a new set of legal fees for probating the Will, plus Court Cost, Appraiser Fees, etc., all of which must be paid out of the value of the estate.

On the other hand, to establish a Revocable Living Trust, it is only required that a proper Declaration Of Trust be prepared which names the Trust Maker (Trustor), the Trust Manager(Trustee), the Trust Manager after the Trust Maker passes (Successor Trustee), the persons who will receive the Trust Property after the death of the Trustor (Beneficiary), a listing of the property to be held In Trust, and the filing or recording of the property transfer instruments.

All of this material is included in this Non-Lawyers Living Trust Kit, and it is designed and presented in such a way that preparation is easy, uneventful and without the need of any legal advice from a lawyer.

Take, for example, the Declaration Of Trust: it essentially requires the completion of a first page which names all of the parties, a second page which requires a listing of the property going into the Trust, and a third page which requires only the naming of the State of residence, and the signature of the trust maker before a Notary Public.

All that is left is for the preparation of the property transfer documents and, depending on the type of property being transferred into the trust, this will be one or more documents. For example, if transferring a home, then you would prepare the Deed Of Realty To Trust; if Stocks or Bonds, then you would prepare the Securities Transfer To Trust, etc. In other words, there is a separate document for each of the different types of property (eight all total).

After you record the property transfer document, if it is required, the Trust is established and you have effectively, with very little time invested, saved your heirs hundreds or even thousands of dollars in future legal fees.

If the previous description of the establishment of a Living Trust seems too simple, rest assured that while it may require additional steps if the property going into the trust is varied and not all locally situated, these additional steps are made simple in this Instruction Guide, and not much more time consuming than simply thinking about it.

This Non-Lawyers Living Trust Kit has simplified the preparation requirements to such an extent that most people purchasing the kit are surprised and elated that they can easily do-it-themselves without incurring any lawyer fees.

The Declaration Of Trust requires a few considerations that the Trust Maker must make, namely, it must be decided how the property will be divided, either equally between the beneficiaries, a fixed percentage to each beneficiary, or specific property to certain of the beneficiaries.

This is all made simple by the professionalized design of the Declaration Of Trust which provides a separate Page 1 for an easy selection of one of these three considerations.

All of the provisions necessary to effectively manage the Trust are predrafted in the Trust Clauses that provide all of the rights and authorities the parties have under the Declaration Of Trust.

And since the Declaration Of Trust is a Revocable Living Trust, this means the Trust Makers are free to deal with their property any way they see fit, without any restrictions. In other words, the Trust Makers can sell, trade, or borrow money against the property, the same as any personally held property, while at the same time, enjoy the peace of mind knowing that, upon passing, the value of their estate will not be depreciated by the probate system.

It is to your advantage to read all of the material included in this Instruction Guide as it is non-legal, but does include some important facts that may be required not only in dealing with the Living Trust, but with other events that occur in everyday living.

And in the eight Chapters that follow, you will receive knowledge that would otherwise cost thousands of dollars in legal fees or many many hours of personal research, even assuming then that a lot of the material is the work product of the author and his staff, and therefore, not readily available to the general public except upon exhaustive inquiry.

To insure the correct preparation of each of the Forms, there are fully illustrated Specimen Forms in the Appendix Section.

Preface

For someone who has suffered through the intolerable delays and high cost of a Probate Action, an appreciation of the 'estate saving' advantages of a Living Trust is substantial.

It was not until 1965 when author Norman F. Dacey a Professional Estate Planner, published his bestseller 'HOW TO AVOID PROBATE' that the general public became consciously aware of the rampant abuses in the Probate System and that the vehicle to avoid these abuses was the 'REVOCABLE LIVING TRUST'.

During the 1970's, there were concerted efforts by many concerned individuals, both professional and non-professional, to draft and instigate the States to adopt legislation to cure the apparent ills of the probate system. One of the leading advocates was the American Bar Association.

It is, however, a well known fact that most long-standing practices by Public Officials are easy to talk about, but difficult to change, thus, making the suggested changes in the various State Probate Laws a difficult and seemingly impossible feat to accomplish.

As a consequence, the changes became known as 'The Uniform Probate Code' which was adopted by twelve States, namely, Alabama, Arizona, Colorado, Florida, Hawaii, Idaho, Minnesota, Montana, Nebraska, New Mexico, North Dakota and Utah.

Many of the State Legislative Bodies, under pressure from their Probate Court Officials, simply refused to adopt the Code. Others who did adopt the code, did so only after emasculating many of the corrective provisions of the draft code.

What this effectively means is that those deplorable probate conditions that existed and prevailed during the previous years had not been laid to rest, but are, in fact, alive and well. Therefore, the only real protection from these probate abuses is to avoid, eliminate or, at the least, minimize the necessity for probate.

There are several ways this can be accomplished, but the most common way is, of course, by acquiring property as Joint Tenants. Of course, the problem with joint tenancy is twofold, first, there must be a survivor and secondly, if both joint tenants die as a result of a common disaster, then the joint tenancy has no application or effect in regards to the heirs of the deceased, thus making probate a requirement.

There are various ways to avoid, eliminate or at least minimize the future prospects of exposing your heirs to the depressive nature of the probate system, all of which are based upon the concept of utilizing one of the various types of Trust. The Inter Vivos or Living Trust, as it is commonly called, is one of those types of trust that can serve as a vehicle to avoid or eliminate probate at very little cost to the trust maker.

While the Living Trust is the least complicated of all of the types of Trust, it offers no tax advantages as do some of the other types of Trust, but it does provide the person or persons making the Trust with the advantage of retaining complete control and freedom over their property during their lifetime, unlike some other types of Trust.

Prior to the publication of Author Dacey's Book, 'HOW TO AVOID PROBATE,' information, counsel and advice regarding a Living Trust was not easy to come by, even from the legal community. This was no surprise because Living Trusts do not generate 'probate fees.'

Even today, most lawyers will not readily offer counsel and advice regarding Living Trusts. The single most offered reason for this failure to offer such advice is that there is not enough legal precedence to support such advice.

There is, of course, another school of thought on that reasoning which dictates that conflicts and controversy have been the exception rather than the rule when it comes to Living Trusts. In other words, the legal profession has not been afforded many opportunities to drag the Living Trust through the Court System and charge those high legal fees which, to this writer, shows GOOD LAW.

One of the key features of any Trust, including the Living Trust, is its ability to be operated, more or less, in a shroud of secrecy. There were aggressive efforts made by some of the drafters of the Uniform Probate Code to strip away the secrecy aspect of a Trust. The end result being that some of the States that did, in fact, adopt the Uniform Probate Code included provisions in the Code which require that a 'Notice Of The Trust' be filed with the appropriate probate body of that jurisdiction.

This Notice Of Trust must provide the names and addresses of the Trustor and Trustees of such Trust. However, in spite of this notice requirement under the Uniform Probate Code, the Living Trust is still substantially a private trust.

One of the real advantages in maintaining this privacy is that it avoids the publicity that arises upon the death of either a prominent citizen of the community or one with a large estate. This kind of publicity provides a good breeding ground for controversy and connivance, something the heirs of the deceased person can well do without.

At any rate, the Chapters that follow will not only enhance your knowledge of the Living Trust, but also provide the means for easily and simply preparing your own Living Trust.

Chapter 1
THE LIVING TRUST

The LIVING TRUST, as it is commonly called is, in fact, an Inter Vivos Trust which means the trust will exist only during the lifetime of the Trust Maker (Trustor). There is an exception to this lifetime provision when the trust is continued after the death of the maker for the benefit of one or more beneficiaries (heirs) by reason of age or other conditions.

The Declaration Of Trust included in this Non-Lawyers Living Trust Kit provides for the continuation of the trust after the death of the Trustor or Trustors either when a beneficiary is under the age of 21 years, or when the distribution of the trust property to certain beneficiaries(heirs) will be made over a period of time and when certain conditions are met.

There are two types of Living Trust, 'Revocable' and 'Irrevocable.' A Revocable Trust is one that can be revoked at any time by the trust maker, while an Irrevocable Trust is one that cannot be revoked without the written consent of the beneficiaries. The Living Trust included in this Kit is a Revocable Living Trust, therefore, all of the material provided in this publication will be directed to a Revocable Living Trust.

Keep in mind that a Revocable Living Trust is a vehicle designed solely to avoid or eliminate the unfortunate delays and high cost of probate. It, however, does not offer any tax advantages, nor does it allow the beneficiaries(heirs) to escape the payment of estate taxes on the gross value of the Trust Property.

What the Living Trust does accomplish, in spite of its lack of any tax advantages, is to provide the maker (Trustor) with a method by which assets accumulated during his(her)lifetime can be transferred to the beneficiaries(heirs) in relative privacy, in a minimum amount of time and at practically no cost (except the cost of recording the necessary instruments in the Public Records).

Even though title to the trust property is in the name of the trustee (who is usually the trustor), no authority or power to wheel and deal with the trust property is thereby lost since any action the trustor could engage in as the sole owner of the property is readily available to him(her) as the trustee under the terms of the Declaration Of Trust.

In other words, the Trustor acting as Trustee, has the right to manage the trust property with absolute discretion, including the right and authority to mortgage, pledge, encumber, improve, lease or sell.

This broad base of authority enjoyed by the trustee under the Declaration Of Trust is manifestly uninhibited since the beneficiary's interest in the trust property is essentially non-existent.

What interest the beneficiaries(heirs) have in the trust property emerges only upon the death of the Trustor or Trustors, whichever the case may be.

In other words, a Living Trust is a vehicle that can be legally operated or legally aborted at the will of the Trustor or Trustors, while fully preserving an estate that will pass to his or her heirs without the necessity of a cumbersome and costly probate.

Chapter 2

THE FUNDAMENTALS OF A TRUST

This chapter will provide definitions and meanings for most of the terms that you will encounter as you gain an understanding as to both the fundamental elements of a trust and as to why certain terms or words are used in the Declaration of Trust, the Trust Instruments and the Trust Forms.

A. THE LEGAL DEFINITION OF A TRUST.

In simple terms, a Trust can best be described as a 'Fiduciary Relationship' that exists when one party (the Trustor) transfers *in Trust* to a second party (the Trustee) title to or legal possession of certain property to be held for the benefit and use of a third party or parties (known as the beneficiary or beneficiaries).

Thus, there legally exist two types of ownership in the entrusted property, namely: (1) Legal title held by the Trustee and (2) an Equitable title held by the beneficiary. And of course, the equitable title held by the beneficiary has no real value until the death of the Trustor or Trustors.

B. THE FUNDAMENTAL TERMS OF A TRUST.

At this point, the fundamental terms associated with a Trust will be defined in alphabetical order:

1. Beneficiary. The beneficiary or beneficiaries are the persons or entities who will receive the trust property upon the death of the trustor or trustors.

2. Declaration Of Trust. The Declaration Of Trust is the formal, written expression by the Trustor creating the Trust. It contains the designation of the parties, the designation and description of the property which will be transferred to the Trust and the terms of the Trust.

3. Entity. An entity is any legally established body, such as a corporation, a trust, a governmental unit, certain partnerships, etc.

4. Fiduciary Relationship. A Fiduciary Relationship exists when it involves a position of confidence and trust.

5. Inalienability. Inalienability in regards to the beneficiary's interest in the trust property means that the beneficiary has no equitable interest in the trust property that can be assigned, sold, pledged, or attached.

6. Irrevocable Trust. An irrevocable trust is a trust that cannot be revoked at will by the trustor without the consent of the beneficiary(ies).

7. Per Stirpes. Per Stirpes is a legal phrase that means if a beneficiary does not outlive (survive) the trustor (in this case), then such beneficiary's share of the trust property will go to his or her heirs. *(See: Survivors of Them)*

8. Revocable Trust. A revocable trust is a trust that can be terminated or revoked at the will of the trustor without consent of the beneficiary(ies).

9. Successor Trustee. The successor trustee is the person named in the trust to assume the duties of the trustee upon the death or disability of the trustor.

10. Survivors Of Them. *Survivors of Them* is a legal phrase that means if a beneficiary does not outlive (survive) the trustor (in this case), then the trust property will be divided between or among the surviving beneficiaries. In other words, the deceased beneficiary's share of the trust property does not pass to his or her heirs.

11. Trustee. The trustee is the person or entity who assumes legal title to the trust property from the trustor in accordance with the expressed provisions of the Declaration of Trust.

12. Trustor. The trustor is the person who, by both expressing an intention to create the trust and subsequently transferring property into the trust, causes the trust to come into existence or be created. The Trustor is sometimes also known as the Assignor, Donor, Grantor, Releasor, Settlor, and Transferor.

13. Trust Res. The trust res is the property or property interest held by the trustee under the trust. In other words, it is the Trust Property.

C. THE FUNDAMENTAL ELEMENTS OF A TRUST.

The four basic elements necessary to establish a valid trust are:

1. There must be an actual and constructive expression either by words or by conduct that the Trustor intends to establish a Trust in respect to some particular property;

2. There must be an identifiable designation of the Trust Property;

3. There must be an actual designation of the parties to the Trust; and

4. There must be a valid Trust Purpose. For example, if the purpose of the Trust is to provide, promote and secure the welfare of your children, then this is a valid Trust Purpose. If however, the purpose is to defraud or hinder a creditor, then this is an invalid Trust Purpose.

D. AN ADDITIONAL ELEMENT OF A TRUST.

There is an additional element that must be present in order for the Trust to come into being, and that is, ". . . there must be an effective, immediate and present transfer of property to the Trustee." In other words, a mere promise to transfer property *in Trust* at some future date will not create or establish a Trust.

An effective transfer means a legally valid transfer or constructive delivery of property to the Trustee.

Chapter 3

WHAT THE KIT PROVIDES

The Non-Lawyers Living Trust Kit provides, in addition to other forms and instruments, an easy to prepare DECLARATION OF TRUST which is revocable at the will of the Trustor(Trustors), and gives the Trustor (Trustors) the option of providing, upon death, for the distribution of the Trust Property under one of three methods, namely: (1) an equal sharing of the trust property between or among all beneficiaries, if there are more than one, (2) giving each beneficiary a fixed percentage of the trust property, and (3) giving certain of the trust property to certain beneficiaries.

To be more specific, the Declaration Of Trust controls and provides for the ultimate distribution of the trust property while allowing the Trustor(s) complete control over all of the property during his, her or their lifetimes.

The Kit also includes the Property Transfer Forms and Instruments necessary to legally transfer title from the Trustor's Name personally, to the Trustor's Name as Trustee under the Trust. This would include the following: (1) Deed of Realty To Trust, (2) Quit Claim Deed To Trust, (3) Financial Account Transfer To Trust, (4) Securities Transfer To Trust, (5) Assignment of Secured Realty Interest To Trust, (6) Chattel Transfer To Trust, (7) Assignment of Contract To Trust, and (8) Business Interest Transfer To Trust.

Other forms are provided which may either be required under State Laws, or necessary to accomplish the objectives of the Trustor(s), namely:

1. NOTICE OF TRUST.

This Form may or may not be required in the State where you plan to establish the Trust. Only a few States require the filing of this NOTICE with the appropriate probate court. *(See: Chapter 5)*

2. LAST WILL AND TESTAMENT.

This Last Will and Testament may be used if there is property that will not be transferred to the Trust or there are minor children who will need a Guardian if the Trustor should pass away before they reach majority age.

3. DISCLAIMER BY SPOUSE.

This Instrument is only required if the Trust is being established by one spouse with property that the other spouse may or may not have an interest in. If, of course, both spouses establish the Trust Jointly, then this instrument is not required.

4. AMENDMENT TO TRUST LIMITING DISTRIBUTION OF ASSETS TO A BENEFICIARY.

This Form is used only if the Trustor(Trustors) decide that certain of the Trust Beneficiaries would not intelligently or competently manage his or her lump sum share of the Trust Property. Therefore, the Trustor can elect how such beneficiary's(ies') share of the Trust Property will be paid out, for example: (1) in monthly, quarterly or annual installments, (2) in installments to a certain date, then the balance paid out in full, (3) when such beneficiary reaches a certain age, or (4) any other condition that the Trustor may elect to impose, for example, upon attaining a College

Degree, entering a marriage, etc. In other words, the possible conditions are endless.

5. RECORDING LOG.

This Form is provided for the purpose of permitting the Trustor and/or Trustee to make a chronological record of each Trust Transaction beginning with the establishment of the Trust and continuing through the execution and recordation of each Form and Instrument pertinent to the operation and management of the Trust.

The importance of completing this Form as the events happen, cannot be too strongly advised since the Successor Trustee may very well need the information entered in this Recording Log to understand what property the Trust holds, what conditions prevail regarding the property, or any other material fact regarding the Trust that needs to be considered.

OVERVIEW

You should, at this point, have a good idea as to what range of options the Trustor may exercise in pursuing the Trust Goals.

Although the presence of the numerous forms in the kit may tend to be overwhelming to some, it is very likely that only a few of the forms will be used in establishing the trust, for example, in the most simple of circumstances, the Declaration of Trust is prepared with Trustor(s) and Trustee(s) being one and the same, the Successor Trustee being one or more of the Beneficiaries, the Beneficiaries being the Trustor(s) Children, and the property going into the Trust being listed on the back of Page 1 (Page 2).

All that remains is the selection, preparation and filing, recording or personally delivering the applicable property transfer forms to the appropriate agency, firm, institution or office to effect the legal transfer of the property to the trust.

While the steps necessary to establish the Living Trust are not quite as simple as preparing a simple one page Will Form, they are however, simple enough to justify the preservation of your estate for your heirs.

Chapter 4

WHAT THE KIT REQUIRES

In the previous Chapter, it was fully outlined as to what this Kit provides in the way of legally establishing the Living Trust and managing its operation and changes. Therefore, this Chapter will briefly discuss what is required of the Trustor to further his, her or their objectives in establishing and maintaining the Trust.

To begin with, it is not required that you see a lawyer to prepare any of the Trust Forms, as they are simply drawn, and even include in the appropriate places, lines to facilitate the use of a writing pen (Black ink).

In addition to this, the legal terminology has been substantially eliminated from the Declaration of Trust, the Trust Forms and Trust Instruments. And what is left is important enough to leave intact, but yet, requires no mental gymnastics on the part of the Trustor to comprehend the meanings.

The only significant legal phrase that appears in any of the forms is the one drafted into the Transfer Instruments which states, "TO HAVE AND TO HOLD . . ." This is a legal clause usually found in the granting portion of a deed or other property transfer instrument which defines both the extent of ownership in the property granted and the intent to transfer it to another forever.

The words "TO HAVE" are the English translation of the Latin Word *Habendum* which means the grantor (the person owning the property) holds absolute or fee simple title to the property to be transferred, whereas, the words "TO HOLD" are the English translation of the Latin Word *Tenendum* which means the grantee (the person who will receive the property) will be conveyed title to the property forever.

This explanation was given for the benefit of those who may entertain a concern as to the exactness of the legal phraseology drafted into the forms.

Once the decision is made to go forward with the Living Trust, the first most important requirement is that the Trustor consider, before preparing any of the Trust Forms, what will be the ultimate objectives of the Trust and how will they be met? For example, while the singular most important objective of the Living Trust is to avoid or eliminate probate, in second place of importance is having the ability to legally accomplish the intents of the first objective.

Now, both of these objectives can only be successfully accomplished when the Trustor(s) considers and decides each of the following: (1) who will be the beneficiaries? (2) who qualifies to be the Successor Trustee? (3) how should the trust property be divided upon the death of the trustor, that is: equally; at a fixed percentage to each beneficiary; or certain property to certain of the beneficiaries?

These are all questions that bear significance upon whether or not the Trust will accomplish what the maker(trustor) intends. Once these issues are resolved, then the preparation of the Declaration of Trust can take place.

Also, it is required that a legally identifiable description of the Trust Property be made in the Property Clause of the Declaration Of Trust. This necessarily means that the legal description (not the street address) of all real property be listed, and serial numbers of any chattel property, or such other description that a reasonable person may use to clearly identify the property from among others of a like kind and nature.

At this point, it should be clearly evident that the requirements of this Kit are few and basic. In fact, the preparation time for the Trust and Property Instruments (not counting time spent commuting to the Recorder's Office or the Bank) is less than one hour.

And if you have never had exposure to Trust terminology, or the mechanics of a Trust, then it is necessary that you take the challenge by spending the time required to read all of the material included in this Instruction Guide, including a review of the illustrated examples of actual Trust Forms and Instruments in the Appendix Section.

The material included in this Instruction Guide is purposely kept brief (as an education in Trust is not a requirement of this Kit) without sacrificing any important factors pertinent to the legal establishment and operation of the Trust.

With this in mind, proceed to the next Chapter (Chapter 5), as it will provide some basic, but helpful information in regards to Community Property Laws, Estate considerations, Estate Taxes, etc.

Chapter 5
GENERAL INFORMATION APPLICABLE TO TRUST

This Chapter will outline several considerations that may play a part in either the establishment, operation or termination of the Living Trust. In particular, these considerations include: (1) Community Property Laws, (2) Curtesy and Dower Laws, (3) Estate Taxes, (4) The Uniform Probate Code, and (5) The Witness Requirements of a Last Will and Testament.

Each of these considerations will be separately outlined and discussed below:

1. COMMUNITY PROPERTY LAWS.

Several of the States have what is generally called *Community Property Laws.* The thrust of these laws is simply that all property acquired during the term of the marriage is community property jointly owned by both spouses, unless one spouse disclaims an interest in any such property.

The consequence of these laws as they affect the legality of property transferred to the Trust is that, if one spouse establishes a Living Trust with property acquired during the marriage, then the other spouse must disclaim an interest in such property in order for the transfer to be valid.

In the case of a Joint Living Trust with both spouses, this is not a problem since both spouses will join in the transfers of property to the Trust.

In those States that do not have Community Property Laws, the rules of law, in regards to property acquired by either or both spouses, are called the laws of *Equitable Distribution.*

What this effectively means is that, while each spouse may separately acquire, sell or otherwise dispose of property acquired during the marriage, all such property bought by either spouse will be subject to an equitable distribution in the event of a divorce or other Judicial Property Settlement.

This can be construed to mean that there is a potential lien held by one spouse against any property transferred to a Trust established by only one of the spouses. Therefore, it is important that even in Non-Community Property States, the Disclaimer by Spouse be utilized.

Listed below are the nine States that presently have Community Property Laws:

Arizona	Louisiana	Texas
California	Nevada	Washington
Idaho	New Mexico	Wisconsin

2. CURTESY LAWS.

Several of the States have laws that affect the right and use of a deceased wife's property by the surviving husband. These laws are called *Curtesy Laws,* and what they grant to a surviving husband is the right to use one-third or more of his deceased wife's real property for as long as he lives, even if the property was previously sold, but he must not have signed the deed nor disclaimed an interest in the property.

Here again, is a compelling example as to why a Disclaimer By Spouse should be properly issued.

Listed below are those States which have Curtesy Laws:

Delaware	Rhode Island
District of Columbia	Tennessee
Hawaii	Vermont
Kentucky	Virginia
Massachusetts	West Virginia
Ohio	Wisconsin

3. DOWER LAWS. Dower Laws have the same effect as Curtesy Laws except that they grant to the surviving wife, the right and use of one-third or more of her deceased husband's real property for as long as she lives, in spite of a prior sale of the property, provided she did not sign the deed nor disclaim an interest in the property.

Listed below, are those States having Dower Laws:

Alabama	Ohio
Delaware	Rhode Island
Florida	South Carolina
Hawaii	Tennessee
Kentucky	Vermont
Massachusetts	Virginia
Michigan	West Virginia
Montana	Wisconsin
New Jersey	

4. ESTATE TAXES. It was previously mentioned that a Living Trust offered no tax advantages, as its single most valuable feature is its avoidance and elimination of probate. However, whenever property passes from a deceased person, that property is considered property of the deceased person's estate, and thereby, becomes subject to both Federal and State Estate Taxes.

Under the current (1992) tax laws, two provisions of the tax laws can apply, that is, (1) the *Unlimited Marital Deduction*, which allows a deceased spouse's estate to pass tax free to the surviving spouse and (2) each deceased spouse's estate may claim an exemption of up to $600,000 of estate value, if the estate is postured in two trust commonly known as the A-B Trust.

The net estate value above $600,000 is subject to Federal Estate Taxes ranging from 37% to 55. These tax rates were adopted by Congress in 1981, under what is called the 1981 Economic Recovery Tax Act, however, there is currently (1993) legislation being considered by the 1993 Congress that will reduce the $600,000 exemption to $200,000.

With a regular living trust, like the one included in this kit, the unlimited marital deduction will apply upon the death of the first spouse, then upon the death of the second spouse, or if the trust was established by a single person, the beneficiaries can claim the up to $600,000 Federal Estate Tax Exemption, provided, however, that the 1993 Congress does not enact legislation that will reduce the $600,000 to $200,000, in which case, the beneficiaries can claim as exempt whatever amounts the tax laws dictate.

There mayb also be State Inheritance Taxes due, depending on the value of the estate and whether or not State Laws allow for the waiver of estate taxes.

If it can be projected that the net estate value will exceed $600,000 (or $200,000 if the law is enacted), then an A-B Trust might be more appropriate than the current Living Trust. Call the publisher for information on the A-B Trust.

5. UNIFORM PROBATE CODE.

Listed below, are the 12 States which adopted, in whole or in part, certain provisions of the Uniform Probate Code. One of the provisions drafted into the Code was the requirement that when a Trust was established, Notice of such Trust must be given to the appropriate Probate Body in the jurisdiction where the Trust is established.

Some States, while adopting the Uniform Probate Code, did not however establish procedures for the filing of a Notice of Trust. Therefore, a Notice Of Trust is not a requirement in those States. To confirm this fact, simply call the Probate Court in the County where you plan to establish the Trust and ask.

The States adopting the Uniform Probate Code are as follows:

Alabama	Hawaii	Nebraska
Arizona	Idaho	New Mexico
Colorado	Minnesota	North Dakota
Florida	Montana	Utah

6. WITNESS REQUIREMENTS FOR A LAST WILL.

A Last Will and Testament is included in this Kit for the purpose of either directing the distribution of property not included in the Living Trust, designating an Executor for such property, and/or designating a Guardian for any minor children of the Trustors.

The Last Will and Testament will not, however, be valid unless properly signed by the number of witnesses required under State Laws, as indicated below:

A. The following States require that a Will be witnessed by at least two (2) witnesses:

Alabama	Delaware	Indiana
Alaska	District of Columbia	Iowa
Arizona	Florida	Kansas
Arkansas	Georgia	Kentucky
California	Hawaii	Louisiana
Colorado	Idaho	Maryland
Connecticut	Illinois	Michigan

Minnesota	North Carolina	Texas
Missouri	North Dakota	Utah
Mississippi	Ohio	Virginia
Montana	Oklahoma	Washington
Nebraska	Oregon	West Virginia
Nevada	Pennsylvania	Wisconsin
New Jersey	Rhode Island	Wyoming
New Mexico	South Dakota	
New York	Tennessee	

B. The following States require that a Will be witnessed by at least three (3) witnesses:

Maine	South Carolina
Massachusetts	Vermont
New Hampshire	

C. Countries other than the United States:

Since the laws of the various Countries, and even those States or Provinces within a Country may vary, it would be wise to consult a Local Counselor or Barrister in regards to the witness requirements of a particular foreign locale.

Chapter 6

DESCRIPTION OF THE TRUST FORMS AND INSTRUMENTS

In this Chapter, the Declaration Of Trust and each of the separate Trust Forms and Instruments will be briefly described as to their respective application in a Living Trust.

Each of the respective Trust Forms, as well as each of the individual pages of the Declaration of Trust have Form Numbers at the bottom center of the page, therefore, all references to the individual forms and pages will be both by Form Number and Titles.

The Declaration Of Trust will be described in its entirety since it is important that the Trustors have a working knowledge of the scope of authority and attendant limitations conferred under the Declaration Of Trust.

Keeping in mind that the Declaration Of Trust is not only the Trustor's manifest expression of his(her)(their) intent to create or establish a Trust with respect to certain property, but also, the Trustor's, Trustee's and Successor Trustee's rights, reservations, conferments and limitations under the Trust.

And since the Declaration Of Trust incorporates eighteen (18) separate Clauses, extending over five (5) pages, each of these Clauses will be separately described as to its application to the Trust.

The description of the Trust Forms and Instruments will be divided into two (2) sections. The first Section will describe each of the Forms and Clauses in the Declaration Of Trust and the second Section will describe all of the other Forms and Instruments included in the Kit.

1. DECLARATION OF TRUST FORMS.

a. FORM AT-101-1. (Page 1 of the Trust) This Form is Page 1 of the Declaration Of Trust, if the Trustor desires that the Trust Property be equally distributed to the beneficiaries, if more than one.

It also provides for: (1) the date of the Trust, (2) the designation of the parties, i.e., Trustor, Trustee, Successor Trustee and Beneficiary(ies), (3) the Trust Intent and Beneficiary Clause which includes a "Per Stirpes" and "Survivors of Them" Clause with regards to the beneficiaries.

b. FORM AT-101-2. (Page 1 of the Trust) This Form is Page 1 of the Declaration Of Trust, if the Trustor desires that the Trust Property be distributed to the beneficiaries at a fixed percentage to each of the beneficiaries, in addition to the other clauses described above under Form AT-101-1.

c. FORM AT-101-3. (Page 1 of the Trust) This Form is Page 1 of the

Declaration Of Trust, if the Trustor desires that certain of the Trust Property be distributed to certain of the beneficiaries, in addition to the Clauses described above under Form AT-101-1.

The Trust Property.

d. FORM AT-102-1. This Form includes Clause 2 of the Declaration Of Trust which provides for the listing of the Trust Property. It also includes a property provision that legally includes in the Trust, any property subsequently acquired by the Trustee. This Form is on the back of both Forms AT-101-1 and AT-101-2.

The Trust Property.

e. FORM AT-102-2. This Form is also Clause 2 of the Trust, and provides for separate designation of the Trust Property to allow the distribution of certain property to certain beneficiaries. Both Trust Property Forms provide that any property later acquired is also legally included in the Trust, even though not shown in this Clause.

f. FORM AT-103. (Page 3 of the Trust) This Form is PAGE 3 of the Declaration Of Trust and it includes TRUST CLAUSES 3 through 8, respectively. A brief description of each of the Clauses is as follows:

Authority, Power and Rights of Trustor(s).

CLAUSE 3. This is a three part Clause which reserves to the Trustor, the right to amend, modify or revoke the Trust; also, the right to appoint and substitute the Trustee and Successor Trustee; and that all amendments, notices or other matters affecting the Trust be in writing.

Trustor's Exclusive Right To Trust Income.

CLAUSE 4. This Clause reserves to the Trustor(s), all of the Trust Income during the Trustor's lifetime. It also provides that no beneficiary shall have a claim upon the Trust Income or profits.

Trustor's Authority To Encumber Trust Property.

CLAUSE 5. This Clause reserves to the Trustor, the right to mortgage, pledge or otherwise encumber the Trust Property.

Power of Trustee(s).

CLAUSE 6. This is a four part Clause which enumerates the discretionary powers granted to the Trustee(s).

Authority of Successor Trustee To Administer the Trust.

CLAUSE 7. This Clause provides for the Successor Trustee to assume active administration of the Trust either upon the death of the Trustor, or the physical or mental disability of the Trustor.

Termination of Successor Trustee's Authority.

CLAUSE 8. This Clause provides for the termination of the Successor Trustee's authority to actively administer the Trust when the Trustor has sufficiently recovered from his or her medical disability.

g. FORM AT-104. (Page 4 of the Trust) This Form is PAGE 4 of the Declaration Of Trust and it includes TRUST CLAUSES 9 through 14, respectively.

Authority of Successor Trustee To Disburse Funds.

CLAUSE 9. This Clause authorizes and empowers the Successor Trustee to disburse whatever funds are necessary to maintain the comfort and welfare when the trustor is disabled as defined under Clause 7.

Authority of Successor Trustee To Continue Trust.

CLAUSE 10. This Clause authorizes the Successor Trustee to continue the Trust, after the death of the Trustor, when the beneficiary has not reached the age of 21 years, and also, pay from the Trust Assets, the maintenance, education or support of such beneficiary.

Inalienability of Beneficiary's Interest In Trust.

CLAUSE 11. This Clause effectively holds that a Beneficiary's interest in the Trust Property (Trust Res) is without any equitable value until the death of the Trustor. In other words, such interest is inalienable, that is, incapable of being sold, surrendered, transferred, mortgaged, or pledged.

Beneficiary's Proportionate Liability For Estate Taxes.

CLAUSE 12. This Clause simply means that each of the Beneficiaries will be liable for his or her share of the estate taxes levied against the Trust Property upon the death of the Trustor or surviving Trustor.

Revocation of Designation of Beneficiary.

CLAUSE 13. This Clause gives the Trustor the right to revoke a Beneficiary Designation or to add a new Beneficiary without prior notice to such beneficiary.

Non-Liability of Third Parties.

CLAUSE 14. This Clause releases all third parties from any liabilities in regards to providing services or performing any duties in the furtherance of the Trust Purpose. This necessarily includes: Bankers, Brokers, Custodial Agents, Real Estate Firms, Medical Personnel, etc.

The importance of this Clause is without parallel since the Trustee may, from time to time, be required to deal with third parties.

h. FORM AT-105. (Page 5 of the Trust). This Form is PAGE 5 of the Declaration Of Trust and it includes TRUST CLAUSES 15 through 18, respectively.

Extension of Trust Powers.

CLAUSE 15. This Clause provides that the Declaration of Trust is binding upon the successors to the Trustor and Trustee.

Bond Requirements.

CLAUSE 16. This Clause provides that the Successor Trustee may serve without Bond, except that, upon the death of the Trustor, the Successor Trustee may be required to post a bond, in a nominal amount, if any beneficiary is under the age of 21 years.

Applicability of State Laws.

CLAUSE 17. This Clause provides for a designation as to which State Laws the Declaration Of Trust shall be construed under.

Saving Clause.

CLAUSE 18. This Clause provides that in the event some Court should invalidate a provision of this Declaration Of Trust, then that would not invalidate the whole Declaration Of Trust. This is commonly known as an escape valve in a contract.

2. TRUST FORMS AND INSTRUMENTS.

i. FORM AT-200a-b, DEED OF REALTY TO TRUST. When real property (real estate) is being transferred into the Trust, this is the proper instrument to accomplish the conveyance. If, however, the property is being *bought* under a *Real Estate Contract,* also known as, an Agreement For Sale of Real Estate or a Real Estate Land Contract, then this is not the proper instrument to effect the transfer. *See, Form AT-201a-b, Quit Claim Deed To Trust.*

If the property has a mortgage or a Deed Of Trust recorded against it, this is still the proper instrument to effect the transfer since title was transferred by deed before the mortgage or Deed of Trust was recorded.

Quit Claim Deed To Trust.

j. FORM AT-201a-b. When the real property being transferred into the Trust is being *bought* under a *Real Estate Contract* or some other form or type of Real Estate Installment Contract where a deed to the property will not be issued until the Real Estate Contract on the property is fully paid off, then this is the proper instrument to transfer the property interest to the Trust.

The legal effect of this type of ownership is simply that the buyer's interest in the property is limited to his or her interest in the contract purchasing the property. In other words, the buyer has an equitable interest in the contract, not fee simple title to the property.

Financial Account Transfer To Trust.

k. FORM AT-202. This Form provides for the transfer of either a Bank Account or Brokerage Account to the Trust, if the Brokerage Account consists of stocks held in the Broker's Name (street name), then this Form should effectively change the status of the account from the Trustor's name personally, to the Trustor as Trustee under the Trust.

Securities Transfer To Trust.

l. FORM AT-203. This Form must be used to effect the legal transfer of Stocks, Bonds, Debentures, Treasury Bills and Notes into the Trust by authorizing the Transfer Agent for such Securities to change the name of the owner personally, to the owner as Trustee.

This form also requires that the signature(s) of the Transferor(s) be guaranteed by an officer of a commercial bank, trust company, or member of the New York Stock Exchange or another National Securities Exchange where Transferor(s) has(have) an active account or signature on file.

When the request is made to transfer the securities, this Form must accompany the Certificate to the broker or transfer agent.

Assignment of Secured Realty Interest.

m. FORM AT-204a-b. When the property being transferred into the Trust is a Seller's Interest in a debt instrument, such as, a Realty Mortgage or Deed of Trust, then this instrument is the proper instrument; however, this Form cannot be used to transfer a Realty Installment Agreement or Land Contract which require a Vendor Deed (available from the publisher, Form AT-209).

Chattel Transfer To Trust.

n. FORM AT-205a-b. This is the proper instrument to effect the legal transfer In Trust of Chattel Property (moveable property), such as: Motor Vehicles, Equipment, Goods, etc.

Assignment of Contract To Trust

o. FORM AT-206. This Form must be used when the property being transferred into the Trust is a Non-Realty Contract, such as a Royalty Contract, a Deferred Commission Contract, an Annuity Contract, etc. The payor under the contract must be provided with a copy of this Form in order to document the change in status from the Payee personally, to the Payee as Trustee under the Trust.

Business Interest Transfer To Trust.

p. FORM AT-207a-b. When the property being transferred In Trust is an interest in an active business organization, such as a sole proprietorship or partnership, then this instrument establishes a record of such transfer.

This instrument can not be used to transfer a corporation interest since ownership of a corporation is evidenced by Shares of Stock, see FORM AT-203.

Notice of Trust.

q. FORM AT-300. This Notice is only required if the State where the Trust will be established has a requirement that such notice be filed with the probate body of the jurisdiction. Only a few such States have this requirement.

Last Will and Testament.

r. FORMS AT-400a-b. This Last Will and Testament is a Simple Will which may be used to direct the distribution of estate property not included in the Declaration of Trust, and also designates a Guardian of any minor child(ren) of the Testator(Testatrix).

Disclaimer By Spouse.

s. FORM AT-500. This Form permits the Trustor's Spouse to disclaim or renounce all legal claims and interest in property being transferred into the Trust either: (1) as sole and separate Property, (2) Property that may be subject to Community Property Laws, and (3) Property that may be subject to the Curtesy and Dower Laws.

Amendment To Trust Enlarging Powers of Trustee(s).

t. FORM AT-600. This Form is only required if the Trustee will engage in business ventures that require evidence of specific authority. For example, if the Trustee will be buying and selling securities of all types, the Stock Broker may require proof of specific authority to transact such trades, therefore this Form fulfills this requirement.

Amendment To Trust Limiting Distribution of Assets To a Beneficiary.

u. FORM AT-601a-b. This Form must be used if the Trustor desires to limit the distribution of the Trust Assets to a certain beneficiary.

Affidavit of Successor Trustee's Authority To Administer Trust.

v. FORM AT-700. This Form, when supported either by the Death Certificate of Trustor or a Medical Certification showing the physical or mental inability of Trustor to manage the Trust, provides the Successor Trustee with authority to administer the Trust.

Medical Certification.

w. FORM AT-701. This Form may be used to provide proof as to the physical or mental condition of Trustor. The medical practitioner may provide his(her) own form for this purpose, if so, disregard this Form.

Affidavit Terminating Successor Trustee's Authority To Administer Trust.

x. FORM AT-702. This Form would, of course, be used when the Trustor recovers from his(her) medical condition and desires to assume control over the Trust.

Recording Log.

y. FORM AT-900. This Recording Log is to be used to keep a sequential record of each Trust transaction that affects the Trust in any way.

Chapter 7

ESTABLISHING AND MAINTAINING THE LIVING TRUST

Now that you have read all of the previous material and possess a working knowledge as to what a Living Trust is all about, you are ready to proceed with the establishment of the Living Trust.

There are certain steps that must be taken to legally establish and maintain the Living Trust. These steps necessarily include: (1) Selecting the Forms, (2) Preparing the Forms, and (3) Filing, Noticing or Recording the Forms.

Since each of the steps require the consideration of factors relevant to either the Trustor's intent or the legal requirements for establishing a Trust, this Chapter will outline these factors by taking a step-by-step approach to the establishment and maintenance of the Living Trust.

The steps required to establish the Living Trust will guide the selection, preparation and filing, noticing and/or recording of the Trust Forms.

All of the Trust Forms described here will be identified both by their Form Numbers and Titles. Also, while the Forms may be handwritten with Black Ink, it is however important that the information entered on the Forms be completely legible in order to eliminate any possible misunderstanding at some future date as to the Trustor's Intent or the description of any property.

STEP 1. THE SELECTION OF THE FORMS AND INSTRUMENTS

1. The Declaration Of Trust Forms

The Declaration Of Trust Forms are those Forms Numbered AT-101-1(Page 1); AT-101-2(Page 1); AT-101-3(Page 1); AT-102-1(Page 2); AT-102-2(Page 2); AT-103(Page 3); AT-104 (Page 4) and AT-105(Page 5).

You will however notice that there are Three (3) Page 1's Numbered AT-101-1; AT-101-2; and AT-101-3. Therefore, at this point, consideration as to how the property will be distributed to the beneficiaries, upon your death, must be exercised, that is, you must decide whether you desire that each beneficiary receive an equal share of the Trust Property, or each receive a fixed percentage of the Trust Property, or each receive certain items or parcels of the Trust Property.

Select below under either a., b., or c., the method which describes your proposed plan of distribution, and select the Declaration Of Trust Forms so designated:

If the method of distribution will be either to One Beneficiary, or

Two or More Beneficiaries equally sharing the Trust Property, then the complete Declaration Of Trust, Pages 1 through 5, will consist of the following FORMS:

FORMS AT-101-1(AT-102-1), Pages 1 and 2; FORMS AT-103(AT-104), Pages 3 and 4; FORM AT-105, Page 5.

b. If the method of distribution will be distributing to each (two or more) Beneficiary, a fixed percentage of the Trust Property, then the complete Declaration Of Trust, Pages 1 through 5, will consist of the following FORMS:

FORMS AT-101-2(AT-102-1), Pages 1 and 2; FORMS AT-103(AT-104), Pages 3 and 4; AT-105, Page 5.

c. If the method of distribution will be distributing to each (two or more) of the Beneficiaries, certain items or certain parcels of property, then the complete Declaration Of Trust, Pages 1 through 5, will consist of the following FORMS:

FORMS AT-101-3(AT-102-2), Pages 1 and 2; FORMS AT-103(AT-104), Pages 3 and 4; FORM AT-105, Page 5.

2. The Property Transfer Forms And Instruments.

After you have assembled the Declaration Of Trust, you next need to select the appropriate Property Transfer Form and/or Instrument. Therefore, depending on the type of property you plan to use to establish the Trust, select below the Property Transfer Form(s) and/or Instrument(s) which apply to the type of property you plan to use to establish the Trust:

a. The Conveyance of Real Property owned in Fee Simple to establish the Trust:

FORM AT-200a-b, Deed Of Realty To Trust, Pages 1 and 2

b. The Release and Remise of a Contract Interest in Real Property to establish the Trust:

FORM AT-201a-b, Quit Claim Deed To Trust, Pages 1 and 2

c. The Transfer of a Bank or Brokerage Account to establish the Trust.

FORM AT-202, Financial Account Transfer To Trust

d. The Transfer of Securities (Stocks, Bonds, Notes, Debentures, etc.) to establish the Trust:

FORM AT-203, Securities Transfer To Trust

e. The Assignment of a Secured Interest in a Real Estate Debt Instrument to establish the Trust (See Section **m** Page 20):

FORM AT-204a-b, Assignment of Secured Realty Interest To Trust, Pages 1 and 2

f. The Transfer of Personal (Chattel) Property to establish the Trust:

FORM AT-205a-b, Chattel Transfer To Trust, Pages 1 and 2

g. The Assignment of a Non-Realty Contract to establish the Trust:

FORM AT-206, Assignment Of Contract To Trust

h. To Transfer a Business Interest to the Trust:

FORM AT-207a-b, Business Interest Transfer To Trust, Pages 1 and 2

i. Optional forms available from the publisher:

FORM AT-208, Deed of Mineral Rights To Trust

FORM AT-209, Vendor Deed To Trust

3. Other Optional or Required Forms.

The Forms listed under this section include those Forms which are either required under the circumstances of Property Ownership, State Laws or at the Option of the Trustor(s).

Review the circumstances below and then decide if your situation either requires one or more of these Forms or that you desire to effect the procedure described, then select the Form indicated:

a. If the State where you plan to establish the Trust requires that a Notice of the Trust be filed with the Probate Court, then select:

FORM AT-300, Notice of Trust

b. If the Trust is established by only One Spouse and the property being Assigned, Deeded or Transferred to the Trust may be subject to a legal claim by the other spouse, then select:

FORM AT-500, Disclaimer By Spouse

c. If there are either Minor Children in the family, or Property that will not be transferred to the Trust, then select:

FORM AT-400a-b, Last Will And Testament

d. If mature wisdom dictates that certain beneficiaries should not receive their share of the Trust Property in a Lump Sum, but in either monthly, quarterly or annual installments; or upon reaching a certain age; or any other condition that may be reasonably imposed, then select:

FORM AT-601a-b, Amendment To Trust Limiting Distribution Of Assets To A Beneficiary, Pages 1 and 2

e. For a written and sequential record of each Trust transaction, select:

FORM AT-900, Recording Log

OVERVIEW

There may, of course, be several Forms which will not apply to your case—if so, simply disregard them and proceed with the preparation of those Forms that do apply to your situation.

STEP 2. THE PREPARATION OF THE FORMS AND INSTRUMENTS

This Step will briefly discuss the facts and information deemed important for the correct preparation of the Forms. However, only those sections of each Form meeting this criterion will be outlined.

1. The Declaration Of Trust Forms.

The Declaration Of Trust Forms generally require only a minimum of preparation assistance since the Forms are designed in such a way that the pertinent facts and information required to be entered on the Forms is substantially self-explanatory.

There are some pertinent facts that may, however, need to be clarified, namely: the Trust Number, the Execution Date, the Spelling of Names, the Beneficiaries, the Beneficiary's Heirship Provisions, the Trust Property, the Applicability of State Laws, the Signature and Acknowledgment requirements.

Each of these pertinent facts will be discussed below under their respective subtitles.

a. The Trust Name and Number.

A Trust Name and Number should be assigned to the Living Trust in order to establish an unquestionable identity. This identity is important because the current popularity of the Living Trust has so escalated their use, that the increased possibility of a misidentification of a Trust in the Public Records is real.

The most common way to devise a Trust Name and Number is from the Last name of the Trustor(s) with a numerical suffix added, for example, for Trustor John James Doe, the Trust Name and Number could be *The Doe Family Trust No. JJD-1,* or Doe Family Trust JJD-1. (The number *1* indicates the first trust for Mr. Doe.)

During the lifetime of many Trustors, more than one Trust is usually established which means, that the second Trust would simply be Numbered with suffix 2, etc.

This is not to say that some other method of devising a Trust Name and Number could not be used, as this is only the author's suggestion.

b. Trust Execution Date.

The Execution Date of the Trust is the date the Trust is signed before a Notary Public, or other Public Officer. In other words, the date should not be entered on the first line of the Trust until the Trust is ready to be signed by the Trustor(s).

c. The Spelling of Names.

The names of all of the parties named in the Trust should be completely spelled out. This, of course, includes: the names of the Trustor(s), the Trustee(s), the Successor Trustee(s), and the Beneficiary(ies).

The importance of this can be seen when considering the likelihood of grandchildren or even great grandchildren having the same names as their grandparents who would be the Trustor under the Trust, therefore, presenting a problem as to the real identity of Beneficiaries named in the Trust.

d. The Beneficiaries.

On Declaration of Trust Form AT-101-1(Page 1), the Beneficiary(Beneficiaries) is(are) simply named without any further reference, except under the *heirship provision* of the Trust Intent and Beneficiary Clause. However, on Trust Forms AT-101-2(Page 1) and AT-101-3(Page 1), there are provisions that apply to each specific Beneficiary.

For example, on Form AT-101-2(Page 1), each Beneficiary will receive a fixed percentage of the Trust Property, upon the death of the Trustor(s). Therefore, this fixed percentage must be entered adjacent to each Beneficiary's Name, with the total of all percentages being 100%.

In the case of Form AT-101-3(Page 1) where each Beneficiary will receive specific items or parcels of the Trust Property, there must be a numerical reference to the Trust Property designated to be distributed to each such Beneficiary.

This Numerical Reference has been provided in the Trust Property Clause which allows the Trustor(s) to list the Trust Property under separate property numbers that will then be entered adjacent to the name of the respective Beneficiary on the line provided.

e. The Beneficiaries' Heirship Provisions.

The Beneficiaries' Heirship Provision, which is included in Clause 1, Trust Intent and Beneficiary Clause, provides three methods for deciding whether that share of the Trust Property which will be distributed to each of the Beneficiary's should: (1) be divided between (or among) the surviving beneficiaries named in the Declaration of Trust, (2) passed through to the heirs of any such Beneficiary, or (3) provide that a certain Beneficiary's share be *per stirpes* and others be *the survivor(s) of them.*

If a Predeceased Beneficiary's share of the Trust Property will not go to his or her heirs (that is, spouse or children), but will be equally divided between (or among) the surviving Beneficiaries, then Check the First Block, *the survivors of them;* but, if a Predeceased Beneficiary's share will go to his or her heirs, then Check the Second Block, *per stirpes;* if, however, the Trustor decides that certain of the Beneficiaries' shares of the Trust Property should be *per stirpes,* while others should be *the survivors of them,* then it is required that you Check the Second Block, *per stirpes,* and then enter on the lines provided, the name(s) of the Beneficiary(ies) whose share(s) of the Trust Property will be *the survivors of them.*

Keep in mind that the Trustor(s) must make this heirship election, otherwise there will be problems encountered by the Successor Trustee when the Trust Property is distributed to the Beneficiaries, upon the death of the Trustor(s).

These problems would, in all likelihood, require the Successor Trustee to subject the Trust to an expensive court action, something the Trust could well do without.

f. The Trust Property.

It is important that a complete, legal and identifiable description of all property being transferred to the Trust be listed on Page 2 of the Declaration of Trust, The Trust Clause.

In the case of Real Property, a Real Property Interest, or a Real Property Secured Interest, the legal description of such property and all pertinent recording data from the Public records must also be listed.

In the case of Chattel or Personal Property, the property should be clearly described with serial numbers, or other identifiable characteristics when possible. Keep in mind that the descriptions of the property listed under this Trust Property Clause must be identical with those descriptions listed on the appropriate Transfer Form or Instrument.

If there is insufficient space to list all of the property being transferred into the Trust, either contact the publisher and request a "Property Continuation Page", or use a plain sheet of paper and title it at the top, "Trust Property Continued," and in the lower right corner write Page 2b.

g. Applicability of State Laws.

(TRUST CLAUSE NO. 17). Enter under this Trust Clause No. 17, the State under whose Laws the Living Trust shall be construed. For example, the Trustor, while a resident of New York, may decide to execute his or her Living Trust while on vacation in California, or elsewhere. Therefore, the execution will be in California, but the Living Trust will be construed under the laws of New York.

h. Signature and Acknowledgment requirements.

The Declaration of Trust must be signed before a Notary Public or other Public Officer in order to be legally executed.

2. The Property Transfer Instruments.

All of the Property Transfer Forms, except Form AT-203, must be signed before a Notary Public on Page 2, if applicable. Form AT-203 requires a Signature Guarantee instead of a Notary Acknowledgment. Also, be sure that you check the block in the middle section of the form and enter the Property designation number, if the property will be numerically designated in Clause No. 2.

Deed Of Realty To Trust.

a. FORM AT-200. This instrument requires the following facts, namely: the County and State where the property is located; the complete legal description of the property; the date the property was first acquired by the Trustor(s); and the County, State and Land Records where the conveyance instrument was recorded. Some States also require that the deed be witnessed by two witnesses.

Quit Claim Deed To Trust.

b. FORM AT-201. This instrument requires the following facts, namely: the County and State where the property is located; the complete legal description of the property; the date the property was first acquired by the Trustor(s); and the County, State and Land Records where the property acquisition contract was recorded. Some States also require that the deed be witnessed by 2 witnesses.

Remember, this Quit Claim Deed To Trust is required only if the Trustor(s) have a buyer's interest in a Real Estate Contract.

Financial Account Transfer To Trust.

c. FORM AT-202. This form requires the following facts: the designation as to the type of account, i.e., Financial or Brokerage; the Account Numbers; and the Name and Address of the Financial Institution or Brokerage Firm.

Securities Transfer To Trust.

d. FORM AT-203. This Form requires: the Certificate Number of Securities; the type of Securities; and the name and address of the issuing corporation and Number of Shares or Denomination.

Assignment Of Secured Realty Interest To Trust.

e. FORM AT-204. This instrument requires the following facts: the designation of the type of Secured Realty Contract by checking the appropriate block; the date of the Secured Realty Contract; and the County, State and Land Records where the Secured Realty

Contract is recorded.

Chattel Transfer To Trust.

f. FORM AT-205a-b. This Form requires a complete description of the property on the lines provided, including any Serial Numbers or other identifying characteristics.

Assignment Of Contract To Trust.

g. FORM AT-206. This Form requires the following facts, namely: the date of the Contract being assigned; the parties to the contract; and a complete description of the Contract considerations.

Business Interest Transfer To Trust.

h. FORM AT-207a-b. This Form requires the following facts, namely: the Name of the Business Organization; the type of Business Organization; whether a sole proprietorship or partnership; and, if a partnership, the percentage of interest.

3. Optional Or Required Forms.

Notice Of Trust

a. FORM AT-300. The preparation of this Form is only required if the State where you plan to establish the Trust has adopted procedures for filing this Notice. Simply call the Probate Court and ask. If it is required, then provide the following facts, namely: the Name and Address of the Probate Court; the Trust Number and Date established; and the Names and Addresses of both the Trustor(s) and Trustee(s).

Last Will And Testament.

b. FORM AT-400a-b. The Last Will And Testament requires the following: the full name of the person making the Will, i.e, Testator or Testatrix, including any other name commonly used; the State of residence; the name(s) of the heir(s); the description of the property being given; the Common Disaster designation as to whether the spouse survived or predeceased the Testator or Testatrix; the survivorship designation as to whether the distribution will be *per stirpes or the survivors of them;* the names of an Executor and alternate Executor; the names of a Guardian and alternate Guardian for any minor child(ren) of the Testator; and the signatures of Testator(Testatrix) and Witnesses.

Disclaimer By Spouse.

c. FORM AT-500. If this Instrument is applicable under the situations described in Chapter 6, then the following is required: the date signed; the name of spouse signing; the relationship to spouse, whether the husband or wife; the name of other spouse; the Trust Number; date of Trust; County and State where property is located; and a complete and legal description of the property.

Amendment To Trust Limiting Distribution.

d. FORM AT-601a-b. This Form is required if the Trustor(s) elects to limit the distribution of the Trust assets to certain Beneficiary(ies).

OVERVIEW

When all of the applicable Forms and Instruments are completed, signed and acknowledged by a Notary Public or other Public Officer, the Filing, Noticing and/or Recording of the Forms is all that remains to effect the legal establishment of the Living Trust.

The next Step outlines the required filing, noticing or recording procedures for the various type of property transfers. Keep in mind that the legal transfer of the property is not complete until the filing, noticing or recording of the Trust Forms and Instruments have been accomplished.

STEP 3. THE FILING, NOTICING AND/OR RECORDING OF THE FORMS AND INSTRUMENTS.

Remember, one of the required elements of a Living Trust is the "immediate and effective" transfer of the property IN TRUST. The word "effective" as used in this instance means, the "Legal Transfer" of the property to the Trust.

To further clarify what is meant by "legal transfer", it is necessary to first consider the type of property being transferred since the legal transfer of different types of property is, in most cases, dissimilar.

It is, therefore, these differences in the legal transfer of property which will be outlined in this Step 3. To simplify this outline, each of the property situations will be discussed as to its requirements of an effective transfer.

A. A Real Property Title or Real Property Interest of Any Type.

This would include all Assignments, Deeds, Releases or Transfers of any Real Property Title or Interest, whether Equity or Debt Interest, except an Agreement for Sale of Real Estate.

An effective transfer of title becomes legally sufficient when the deed or assignment is recorded in the Public Records. In this instance, this would include the following instruments:

FORM AT-200a-b, Deed Of Realty To Trust, Pages 1 and 2
FORM AT-201a-b, Quit Claim Deed To Trust, Pages 1 and 2
FORM AT-204a-b, Assignment Of Secured Realty Interest To Trust, Pages 1 and 2
FORM AT-500, Disclaimer By Spouse.

B. A Chattel Or Personal Property Interest.

This would include the transfer of title or the physical possession of any type of Chattel or Personal Property. An effective transfer is dictated by State Laws, for example, if the Chattel Property is a Motor Vehicle or Mobile Home, then the Registration or Title must be transferred in accordance with the Motor Vehicle Laws. In such case, the Form AT-205a-b would be used to establish a record of the Trustor's Intent to transfer Title and it may or may not be required by the Motor Vehicle Department.

If however, the property is personal property such as: Household Furnishings, Goods, Equipment, Jewelry, Pets, Sporting Goods, etc., then it is legally sufficient to simply prepare the Form AT-205a-b, and together with the Declaration Of Trust, keep and file as Trust Records in a safe place.

In some jurisdictions, Chattel Transfers can be recorded in the Public Record. This is an option that is left to the discretion of the Trustor(s). If the Chattel Property is of substantial value, then it may be wise to record the Form AT-205a-b in the Public Records.

C. A Bank Account Interest.

There are two ways to accomplish the legal transfer of a Bank Account to the Trust, namely:

1) By Closing. By closing all (or the pertinent) existing accounts and opening new accounts with yourself (yourselves) as Trustee(s).

The Bank will probably need a copy of the Declaration of Trust and the Financial Account Transfer (Form AT-202) which will designate the Trustee's Authority under the Trust and the amount being transferred into the Trust.

2) By Transferring. By transferring the status of the account from you as an individual, to you as Trustee under that certain Declaration of Trust. This can be accomplished in the same manner as adding another person to your account or changing your name on the account.

The Bank will probably need the Trust and Transfer Form as previously described above under Paragraph 1.

D. A Brokerage Account Interest. Since a Brokerage Account can be held in three different ways, i.e., (1) all Securities, (2) all Cash, or (3) a combination of Cash and Securities, the procedures for transferring the account(s) under each of these conditions will be separately outlined below:

1) All Securities. This discussion will assume that the Securities are being held in the Broker's Name (also known as the Street Name), if so, then it is simply a matter of requesting the Broker to issue the Certificates in your name as Trustee (see Section E below).

It will also be assumed that the Securities are fully paid for and the account is not a margin account (otherwise, see Paragraph 3 below).

Assuming the above assumptions apply to your situation, the procedure to follow in transferring the account is simply to present to your Broker, copies of the Declaration of Trust and the Financial Account Transfer Form AT-202 and request that your account be changed to indicate ownership in your name as Trustee(s).

If the Broker will not, does not, or can not comply with your request, then you should either request that the Certificates be issued in your name (then proceed as outlined under Section E below), or find another Broker who will honor your request and have him order your Certificates from the non-cooperating Broker.

While considering these hassles, it may be wise to change your account now, because any difficulties you may experience now, may well be indicative of the difficulties your beneficiaries might experience after your passing.

2) All Cash. This condition may exist for any number of reasons, but the most prevailing reason occurs when the Securities are liquidated in an active account and the investor is more or less sitting on the sidelines awaiting new investment opportunities.

And since the account is all cash, you simply request that the account be changed to indicate you as Trustee. A copy of the Form AT-202 should be given to the Broker at the time the request is made.

If, for some reason, the Broker will not, does not or can not comply with your request, simply demand your cash and go elsewhere. And as mentioned previously, the difficulties you are now experiencing may be indicative of what your beneficiaries will experience after you have passed.

3) Securities And Cash.

This usually occurs in an inactive account which may or may not be a Margin Account.

If it is a Margin Account, it usually means that certain trades did not use up the full amount of the deposit in the account, or simply that the securities bought were less than the amount on deposit. At any rate, the securities are in all likelihood in the Broker's Name, therefore, you will have to either request that the account be changed to your name as Trustee, or do as previously described in both Paragraphs 1 and 2 above.

E. Securities Personally Held.

This would include any Stocks, Bonds, Debentures, or other debt or equity Certificates which are currently registered in your name personally.

To accomplish the legal transfer of these Certificates, simply complete the transfer section on the back of the Certificate, and forward the Certificate, together with the Form AT-203, to the Transfer Agent who issued the Certificate.

If you do not know the name and address of the Transfer Agent, contact the Broker or Banker who arranged the purchase of the Certificates and obtain this information from them.

F. A Non-Realty Contract Interest.

Since a Non-Realty Contract is usually not recorded in the Public Records, an effective transfer becomes legally sufficient when the party executing the contract receives the Assignment Form AT-206, and acknowledges the same, preferably in writing. In other words, although possible, it is not necessary to record this type of Trust Action in the Public Records.

G. A Business Interest.

The effective transfer of a Business Interest necessarily depends on the type of business organization, i.e., Sole Proprietorship or Partnership. Each will be discussed in depth under the subtitles below:

1) Sole Proprietorship.

If the business is a sole proprietorship, it is only necessary to effect changes in the Business Licenses, Bank Accounts, Tradename, etc.

If the Tradename is properly registered with a State or Governmental Agency, then such agency should be notified as to a change in ownership. This is usually accomplished by an assignment of the Tradename. If the business is marketing Patented or Copyrighted products, then the Patents and Copyrights should be assigned to you as Trustee.

The Form AT-207a-b serves as Notice to those individuals and entities affected by the change in legal ownership of the business. Therefore, copies of the Form should be served upon those directly affected.

2) Partnership.

When the business is a Partnership, there are certain legal considerations that must be addressed before a partner in a partnership can be replaced by a Trust.

The first such consideration is whether or not, under State Laws, a Trust can legally become a partner; the Second is whether the transfer of a partner's interest in a partnership effectively terminates the partnership. Both of these considerations require an in-depth review of State Laws, something this Kit can not provide. Therefore, it is essential that Legal Counsel be consulted in order that both of these partnership considerations be properly addressed.

If such counsel determines that a Trust can be a legal partner, then it is simply a matter of proceeding with the establishment of the Trust as outlined under this Chapter. If however, counsel should determine that a Trust can not legally be a partner in a partnership, or that the transfer of a general partner's interest legally terminates the partnership, then you must reconsider your plan to transfer IN TRUST your partnership interest.

H. Notice Of Trust.

If this notice is required in the State where you plan to establish the Trust, you must file it with the Probate Court in the County of such State. Otherwise, simply disregard the Notice, as it has no legal effect if it is not required.

I. Last Will And Testament.

The Last Will And Testament is usually kept in the personal files of the person making the Will, however, some Probate Courts allow the filing of a Last Will, therefore, you will need to call the Court and ask if they have provisions for filing a Last Will And Testament. In no case, should the Last Will be kept in a Safety Deposit Box, as Last Wills are generally not read until after the burial ceremonies.

Chapter 8
POST TRUST ACTIONS

This chapter will briefly review some of the actions that may be either desired or required after the Trust has been established, and the Forms available to accomplish these actions. This would include both voluntary and involuntary actions by the Trustee, or Successor Trustee.

Some of the Forms described below are not included in this Kit, but they may be obtained from the publisher at a very modest cost to cover mailing.

A. These actions effectively amend the Trust under each of the five circumstances outlined below:

1. Enlarging the powers of the Trustee(s) for more specific acts under the Trust:

   FORM AT-600, ENLARGING THE POWERS OF THE TRUSTEE

2. Limiting lump sum payments to a Beneficiary:

   FORM AT-601, AMENDMENT TO TRUST LIMITING DISTRIBUTION OF ASSETS TO A BENEFICIARY

3. Removing a Beneficiary from the Trust:

   FORM AT-610, AMENDMENT TO TRUST REVOKING A BENEFICIARY DESIGNATION

4. Adding a new Beneficiary:

   FORM AT-611, AMENDMENT TO TRUST ADDING A NEW BENEFICIARY

5. Changing the Trustee designation:

   FORM AT-612, AMENDMENT TO TRUST SUBSTITUTING TRUSTEE

6. Changing the Successor Trustee:

   FORM AT-613, AMENDMENT TO TRUST SUBSTITUTING SUCCESSOR TRUSTEE.

7. Adding a Co-Successor Trustee:

   FORM AT-614, AMENDMENT TO TRUST ADDING SUCCES SOR CO—TRUSTEE.

8. Restricting the power of Successor Trustee:

   FORM AT-615, AMENDMENT TO TRUST RESTRICTING POWER AND AUTHORITY OF SUCCESSOR TRUSTEE.

9. Blank Form for amending the Trust:

   FORM AT-616, AMENDMENT TO TRUST.

10. Changing the Successor Trustee:

    FORM AT-617, AMENDMENT TO TRUST ENLARGING POWER AND AUTHORITY OF SUCCESSOR TRUSTEE.

B. These Forms allow the Trustee or Successor Trustee to assign, convey or transfer Property out of the Trust to a Third Party or Beneficiary(ies) whichever is applicable:

1. **FORM AT-650, Trustee's Deed of Realty**
2. **FORM AT-651, Trustee's Quit Claim Deed**
3. **FORM AT-652, Trustee's Financial Account Transfer**
4. **FORM AT-653, Trustee's Securities Transfer**
5. **FORM AT-654, Trustee's Assignment of Secured Realty Interest**
6. **FORM AT-655, Trustee's Chattel Transfer**
7. **FORM AT-656, Trustee's Assignment of Contract**
8. **FORM AT-657, Trustee's Business Interest Transfer**
9. **FORM AT-658, Trustee's Vendor Deed**
10. **FORM AT-659, Trustee's Deed of Mineral Rights**

Keep in mind that upon the death of the Trustors, these Forms (whichever applicable) must be used by the Successor Trustee to Transfer the Trust Property to the Beneficiaries.

C. These Forms allow the Successor Trustee to take charge of the Trust if the Trustor becomes physically or mentally incapacitated: (The following three forms are included in this Book)

1. **FORM AT-700, Affidavit of Successor Trustee's Authority To Administer Trust**
2. **FORM AT-701, Medical Certification** (supporting Form AT-700)
3. **FORM AT-702, Affidavit Terminating Successor Trustee's Authority To Administer Trust**

D. This Form allows the Trustor, Trustee or Successor Trustee to Revoke and Terminate the Trust:

1. **FORM AT-800, Revocation of Trust.**

CONCLUSION

All of the Forms included in this Kit, including those Forms described and listed here may be obtained from the Publisher at a cost of 55¢ each (which includes shipping) or $7.50 for the entire set of Forms.

The author and Publisher wish to extend to you our sincere thanks for selecting this Non-Lawyers Living Trust Kit. We are confident that the Kit will satisfactorily serve your needs.

Please feel free to call or write us if you have any comments, questions or suggestions regarding this Kit or any other do-it-yourself legal kit which we publish. We can provide you with a free Descriptive Brochure which describes the application and use of each of the Non-Lawyer Kits.

APPENDIX A

SPECIMEN FORMS

This Appendix A includes fully prepared Specimen illustrations of each of the LIVING TRUST Forms included in this book.

INDEX TO APPENDIX

FORM AT-101-1

PAGE 1 OF THE DECLARATION OF TRUST

An example of Page 1 of the TRUST with Husband and Wife Trustors; 3 Beneficiaries, each receiving an equal share of the Trust Property, per stirpes, and with joint Successor Trustees;

DECLARATION OF TRUST

(Inter Vivos)

[Trust Name (Number) DOE FAMILY TRUST NO. D-1]

This DECLARATION OF TRUST made and executed this 1ST day of FEBRUARY, 19 92, in the CITY of TUCSON, State of ARIZONA, by and between, the herein named Trustor(s) and Trustee(s):

Trustor		Trustor
Name: JOHN LARSEN DOE	(and)	Name: SALLY LOIS DOE
Address: 123 ANY STREET		Address: 123 ANY STREET
TUCSON, AZ 85700		TUCSON, AZ 85700

Trustee		Trustee
Name: JOHN LARSEN DOE	(☐ and)(☒ or)	Name: SALLY LOIS DOE
Address: 123 ANY STREET		Address: 123 ANY STREET
TUCSON, AZ 85700		TUCSON, AZ 85700

Successor Trustee		Successor Trustee
Name: FRANKLING G. DOE	(☒ and)(☐ or)	Name: DOROTHY A. ROE
Address: 456 MY STREET		Address: 789 YOUR STREET
LOS ANGELES, CA 95000		DENVER, CO 80000

BENEFICIARY (BENEFICIARIES)

Name of Beneficiaries	Name of Beneficiaries
FRANKLIN G. DOE	
DOROTHY A ROE	
JOHN LARSEN DOE, JR.	

WITNESSETH:

1. TRUST INTENT AND BENEFICIARY SURVIVORSHIP CLAUSE.

The Trustor(s) has(have) caused the transfer of all of his(her)(their) rights, title and interest in and to the property herein described in Clause No. 2 of this Declaration of Trust, to the above named Trustee(s) to be held In Trust for the use, benefit and enjoyment of the above named Beneficiary(Beneficiaries) in equal shares, and unless otherwise hereinafter designated, said shares shall be (check one) ☐ the survivor(s) of them or ☒ per stirpes, (excepting for that(those) share(s) of the Trust Property under this Trust to be distributed to Beneficiary(ies), N/A,

if he(she)(they) shall not survive me(us), shall be distributed as follows: N/A.

FORM AT-101-2

PAGE 1 OF THE DECLARATION OF TRUST

An example of Page 1 of the TRUST with Husband and Wife Trustors; 3 Beneficiaries each receiving a fixed percentage of the Trust Property; their shares are per stirpes, except one Beneficiary's Share will go only to the children; and there are alternate Successor Trustees.

DECLARATION OF TRUST

(Inter Vivos)

[Trust Name (Number) DOE FAMILY TRUST NO. D-1]

This DECLARATION OF TRUST made and executed this 1ST day of FEBRUARY, 19 92, in the CITY of TUCSON, State of ARIZONA, by and between, the herein named Trustor(s) and Trustee(s):

Trustor		Trustor
Name: JOHN LARSEN DOE	(and)	Name: SALLY LOIS DOE
Address: 123 ANY STREET		Address: 123 ANY STREET
TUCSON, AZ 85700		TUCSON, AZ 85700
Trustee		**Trustee**
Name: JOHN LARSEN DOE	(☐ and)☒ or)	Name: SALLY LOIS DOE
Address: 123 ANY STREET		Address: 123 ANY STREET
TUCSON, AZ 85700		TUCSON, AZ 85700
Successor Trustee		**Successor Trustee**
Name: HAROLD O. PRICE	(☐ and)☒ or)	Name: WILLIAM P. MANN
Address: 4500 E. SPEEDWAY, S-31		Address: 4500 E. SPEEDWAY, S-31
TUCSON, AZ 85712		TUCSON, AZ 85712

BENEFICIARIES

Names of Beneficiaries	Percentage	Names of Beneficiaries	Percentage
FRANKLIN G. DOE	50 %		%
DOROTHY A. ROE	25 %		%
JOHN L. DOE, JR	25 %		%
	%		%

WITNESSETH:

1. TRUST INTENT AND BENEFICIARY SURVIVORSHIP CLAUSE.

The Trustor(s) has(have) caused the transfer of all of his(her)(their) rights, title and interest in and to the property herein described in Clause No. 2 of this Declaration of Trust, to the above named Trustee(s) to be held In Trust for the use, benefit and enjoyment of the above named Beneficiary(Beneficiaries) who are individually designated to receive a specific and fixed percentage of the Trust Res, as indicated above under the Percentage Column; and unless otherwise hereinafter designated, said share(s) shall be (check one) ☐ the survivor(s) of them, or ☒ per stirpes, excepting for that(those) share(s) of the Trust Property under this Trust to be distributed to Beneficiary(ies), DOROTHY A. ROE

_______________,

if he(she)(they) shall not survive me(us,), shall be distributed as follows: EQUALLY TO THE CHILDREN OF DOROTHY A ROE, NAMELY: ALICE R. ROE, RICHARD L. ROE AND PAT S. ROE

 FORM AT-101-2 Page 1

FORM AT-101-3

PAGE 1 OF THE DECLARATION OF TRUST

An example of Page 1 of the TRUST with Husband and Wife Trustors; 3 Beneficiaries each receiving specific Trust Property; their shares are the survivors of them, and there is one Successor Trustee.

DECLARATION OF TRUST

(Inter Vivos)

[Trust Name (Number) DOE FAMILY TRUST NO. D-1]

This DECLARATION OF TRUST made and executed this 1ST day of FEBRUARY, 19 92 , in the CITY of TUCSON, State of ARIZONA, by and between, the herein named Trustor(s) and Trustee(s):

Trustor		Trustor
Name: JOHN LARSEN DOE	(and)	Name: SALLY LOIS DOE
Address: 123 ANY STREET		Address: 123 ANY STREET
TUCSON, AZ 85700		TUCSON, AZ 85700

Trustee		Trustee
Name: JOHN LARSEN DOE	(☐ and)(☒ or)	Name: SALLY LOIS DOE
Address: 123 ANY STREET		Address: 123 ANY STREET
TUCSON, AZ 85700		TUCSON, AZ 85700

Successor Trustee		Successor Trustee
Name: FRANKLIN G. DOE	(☐ and)(☐ or)	Name:
Address: 456 MY STREET		Address:
LOS ANGLES, CA 95000		

BENEFICIARIES

Names of Beneficiaries	Trust Property Number	Names of Beneficiaries	Trust Property Number
FRANKLIN G. DOE	1		
DOROTHY A. A. ROE	2		
JOHN L. DOE, JR.	3		

WITNESSETH:

1. TRUST INTENT AND BENEFICIARY SURVIVORSHIP CLAUSE.

The Trustor(s) has(have) caused the transfer of all of his(her)(their) rights, title and interest in and to the property herein described in Clause No. 2 of this Declaration of Trust, to the above named Trustee(s) to be held IN TRUST for the use, benefit and enjoyment of the above named Beneficiary(Beneficiaries) who is(are) individually designated to receive certain and specific shares of TRUST RES, as indicated above under the Trust Property Number column; and unless otherwise hereinafter designated, said share(s) shall be (check one) ☒ the survivor(s) of them, or ☐ per stirpes, excepting for that(those) share(s) of the TRUST PROPERTY under this TRUST to be distributed to Beneficiary(ies), ________,

if he(she)(they) shall not survive me(us,), shall be distributed as follows: ________

 FORM AT-101-3 Page 1

FORM AT-102-1

PAGE 2 OF THE DECLARATION OF TRUST

An example of Page 2 of the TRUST, the TRUST PROPERTY CLAUSE when Page 1 is either Form AT-101-1 or AT-101-2, which list eleven separate items of property being transferred to the Trust. At the end of each property description is the number of the form required to transfer that particular property to the Trust.

2. TRUST PROPERTY CLAUSE.

(a) The property being initially transferred by the Trustor(s) to establish this DECLARATION OF TRUST is situated and described as follows: (Describe separately each item of property and its situate, i.e., City, County, State, etc.)

(1) REAL PROPERTY: LOT 24, BLOCK 30, TUCSON VALLEY ESTATES AS RECORDED IN PIMA COUNTY, ARIZONA, IN BOOK 378, AT PAGE 37-43. FORM AT-200a-b

(2) REAL PROPERTY INTEREST: LOT 2, BLOCK 4, CHERRY SUBDIVISION, AS RECORDED IN IN DENVER COUNTY, COLORADO, IN BOOK 4889, AT PAGES 382-400 FORM AT-201a-b

(3) ALL SUMS ON DEPOSIT IN BANK ACCOUNTS NUMBERED 238-2829, 431-8338 AND 345-2929, AT MOUNTAIN NATIONAL BANK, TUCSON, ARIZONA. FORM AT-202

(4) ALL SUMS ON DEPOSIT IN BROKERAGE ACCOUNT NO. MC128743 AT MERRILL, STREET AND COMPANY, DENVER, COLORADO. (FORM AABT-202); FORM AT-202

(5) 5,000 SHARES OF STAND OIL OF CALIFORNIA COMMON STOCK. FORM AT-203

(6) REGISTERED LIMITED PARTNERSHIP INTEREST IN VALLEY FINANCIAL GROUP, CERTIFICATE NO. K-43200, DATED OCTOBER 1, 1989. FORM AT-203

(7) BENEFICIAL INTEREST IN DEED OF TRUST, DATED APRIL 18, 1989, AND RECORDED IN THE OFFICE OF THE PIMA COUNTY RECORDER, IN DOCKET 5066. FORM AT-204

(8) 1990, BUICK REGAL, SERIAL NO. GMC0374123N015. FORM AT-205

(9) ALL HOUSEHOLD FUNISHINGS, APPLIANCES AND EFFECTS IN THE FAMILY RESIDENCE SITUATED AT 123 ANY STREET, TUCSON, ARIZONA. FORM AT-205

(10) ROYALTY CONTRACT DATED JULY 22, 1983, EXECUTED BY ALAMO INDUSTRIAL SUPPLIES, INC., IN FAVOR OF JOHN LARSEN DOE. FORM AT-206

(11) THE SOLE PROPRIETORSHIP INTEREST IN DOE COMPUTER SALES AND SERVICE, LOCATED AT 1099 COMPUTER LANE, SAN DIEGO, CALIFORNIA FORM AT-207

including any other real and/or personal property of every kind and nature which the Trustee(s) may, pursuant to any of the provisions hereof, at any time hereafter acquire, hold or cause to be made payable to this Trust, and the investments and reinvestments (all such property being hereinafter referred to collectively as the Trust Property) for the benefit, purposes and uses, and upon the terms and conditions herein set forth.

FORM AT-102-2

PAGE 2 OF THE DECLARATION OF TRUST

An example of Page 2 of the TRUST, the TRUST PROPERTY CLAUSE when Page 1 is Form AT-101-3, which list three separate designations of Trust Property.

2. TRUST PROPERTY CLAUSE.

(a) The property being initially transferred by the Trustor(s) to establish this DECLARATION OF TRUST is situated and described as follows: (Describe separately each item of property and its situate, i.e., City, County and State):

Trust Property No. 1: (1) LOT2, BLOCK 4, CHERRY MOUNTAIN SUBDIVISION, DENVER COUNTY, COLORADO, RECORDED IN BOOK 4889 OF MAPS AND PLATS AT PAGES 382-383; (2) ALL SUMS ON DEPOSIT IN BROKERAGE ACCOUNT NO. MC128743 AT MERRILL, STREET AND COMPANY; DENVER, COLORADO; (3) ROYALTY CONTRACT DATED JULY 22, 1983, EXECUTED BY ALAMO INDUSTRIAL SUPPLIES, INC. IN FAVOR OF JOHN LARSEN DOE;

Trust Property No. 2: (1) LOT 24, BLOCK 30, TUCSON VALLEY ESTATES, PIMA COUNTY, ARIZONA, RECORDED IN BOOK 378 OF MAPS AND PLATS, PAGES 37-43; (2) ALL HOUSEHOLD FURNISHINGS AND EFFECTS IN THE FAMILY RESIDENCE AT 123 ANY STREET, TUCSON, ARIZONA; (3) 1990 BUICK REGAL, SERIAL NO. GMC037412N015; (4) ALL SUMS ON DEPOSIT IN BANK ACCOUNTS NUMBERED 238-2829, 431-8338 AND 345-2929 AT MOUNTAIN NATITAL BANK, TUCSON, ARIZONA;

Trust Property No. 3: (1) 5,000 SHARES OF STANDARD OIL OF CALIFORNIA COMMON STOCK; (2) BENEFICIAL INTEREST IN DEED OF TRUST DATED APRIL 18, 1989, RECORDED IN PIMA COUNTY RECORDER IN DOCKET 5066; (3) THE SOLE PROPRIETORSHIP INTEREST IN DOE COMPUTER SALES AND SERVICE LOCATED AT 1099 COMPUTER LANE, SAN DIEGO, CALIFORNIA; (4) REGISTERED LIMITED PARTNERSHIP INTEREST IN VALLEY FINANCIAL GROUP, REPRESENTED BY CERTIFICATE NO. 1092, DATED OCTOBER 1, 1989.

Trust Property No. 4: ______

including any other real and/or personal property of every kind and nature which the Trustee(s) may, pursuant to any of the provisions hereof, at any time hereafter acquire, hold or cause to be made payable to this Trust, and the investments and reinvestments (all such property being hereinafter referred to collectively as the Trust Property) for the benefit, purposes and uses, and upon the terms and conditions herein set forth.

FORM AT-102-2 Page 2

FORM AT-103

PAGE 3 OF THE DECLARATION OF TRUST

An example of Page 3 of the TRUST, providing TRUST CLAUSES Numbered 3 through 8.

3. AUTHORITY, POWER AND RIGHTS OF TRUSTOR(S).

(a) The Trustor(s) reserve(s) unto himself(herself)(themselves) the authority, power and right to amend, modify or revoke the TRUST hereby created. No prior notice to or consent of any Beneficiary or the Trustee(s) shall be required.

(b) The Trustor(s) may at any time appoint, substitute or otherwise change the person(s) designated to act as Trustee(s) or successor Trustee under this TRUST hereby created. No prior notice to or consent of any such Trustee, Successor Trustee or Beneficiary shall be required.

(c) All amendments, notices or other instruments effecting or furthering the purposes of this Declaration of Trust, brought pursuant to this Section, shall be in writing and upon proper form.

4. TRUSTOR(S) EXCLUSIVE RIGHT TO TRUST INCOME.

The Trustor(s) during his(her) lifetime, shall be exclusively entitled to all income accruing from the Trust property. No beneficiary named herein shall have any claim upon such Trust Income or profits.

5. TRUSTOR(S) AUTHORITY TO ENCUMBER TRUST PROPERTY.

The Trustor(s), in his(her)(their) capacity as Trustee(s) shall be empowered with the discretionary authority to mortgage, pledge, hypothecate or otherwise encumber with a lien any or all of the Trust Property. Said lien(liens) may be satisfied, settled or discharged from the income, rents or profits accruing from the Trust Property, or any other non-trust property owned by the Trustor(s), if he(she)(they) so elect.

6. POWERS OF TRUSTEE(S).

(a) The Trustee(s) under this Declaration of Trust has(have) all of the discretionary powers deemed necessary and appropriate to administer this trust, including, but not limited to, The power to buy, sell, trade, deal, encumber, mortgage, pledge, lease or improve the Trust Property whether real or personal in nature including every type and nature of both debt and equity instruments, option contracts and/or limited partnership interest, when such action is deemed to be in the best interest and furtherance of the Trust purposes.

(b) In the event this Declaration of Trust provides for more than one Trustee(Co-Trustee), the exercise of any and all authorities, powers and rights accorded to said Trustees under this Trust shall not be construed as requiring the Trustees to act in unison in order to exercise any Trust Power, but that each such Trustee may severally exercise any of the enumerated Trust Powers.

(c) In the event of a physical or mental incapacity or death of one of the Co-Trustees, the survivor shall continue as the Sole Trustee with full authority to exercise all of the powers accorded to a Trustee under this Trust.

(d) The Trustee(s) shall be fully authorized to pay over or disburse to the Trustor(s), any amounts requested by said Trustor(s) from the income or principal of the Trust, from time to time.

7. AUTHORITY OF SUCCESSOR TRUSTEE TO ADMINISTER THE TRUST.

(a) The Successor Trustee shall, upon either the death of the Trustor, the simultaneous deaths of the Co-Trustors, or the death of the surviving Co-Trustor, assume the active administration of this Trust, and forthwith, transfer all right, title and interest in and to the Trust property unto the Beneficiaries, subject however to the provisions of Paragraph 10 below.

(b) The Successor Trustee shall assume the active administration of this Trust during the lifetime of the Trustor(s) when the Trustor or Trustors is(are) unable to actively and competently exercise any of the authorities, powers or rights so accorded under this Trust by reason of a sustaining Medical or Mental Impairment, as Certified by a competent attending medical authority.

8. TERMINATION OF SUCCESSOR TRUSTEE'S AUTHORITY.

The Successor Trustee's authority and power as provided under Paragraph 7(b) may be subsequently terminated by the Trustor(s) without the consent of or prior notice to said Successor Trustee when the Trustor or Trustor(s) is(are) sufficiently recovered from the Medical or Mental impairment as described under Paragraph 7(b) above, and thus, fully and competently capable of actively administering this Trust.

The termination of the Successor Trustee's authority to actively administer this Trust under Paragraph 7(b) shall be effective immediately upon the Successor Trustee's receipt of the Trustor's Notice Terminating all such authorities and powers previously granted by the Trustor(s).

FORM AT-104

PAGE 4 OF THE DECLARATION OF TRUST

An example of Page 4 of the TRUST, providing TRUST CLAUSES Numbered 9 through 14(a).

9. AUTHORITY OF SUCCESSOR TRUSTEE TO DISBURSE FUNDS.

The Successor Trustee shall be fully authorized to pay or disburse such sums from the income or principal as may be required, necessary or desirable to maintain the comfort and welfare of the Trustor(s) when the conditions described in Paragraph 7(b) of this Declaration Of Trust prevails.

10. AUTHORITY OF SUCCESSOR TRUSTEE TO CONTINUE TRUST.

(a) The Successor Trustee shall hold in Continuing Trust, upon the deaths of the Trustor or the surviving Trustors, that share of a beneficiary's Trust Assets when such beneficiary (benefiaries) shall not have attained the age of 21 years. During such period of continuing Trust, the successor Trustee, in his(her) discretion, may retain the specific Trust Property in question, if it is deemed to be in the best interest of the beneficiary(beneficiaries) so to do, or the specific Trust Property may be sold or otherwise disposed of with the proceeds of such sale being invested or reinvested in a reasonably prudent manner.

If said specific Trust Property shall be productive of income, or if such property be sold or otherwise disposed of, the Successor Trustee may pay, disburse or otherwise expend any or all of the income or principal accruing from such property toward the maintenance, education or support of such beneficiary without the intervention of any parent or guardian, and without application to any Court.

Said payments may be made either to the parents, guardian or any other person or institution exercising the responsibility of maintaining, educating or supporting such beneficiary and without any liability upon the Successor Trustee as to the application thereof.

(b) In the event said beneficiary survives the Trustor(s), but dies before attaining the age of 21 years, the Successor Trustee shall transfer, pay over and deliver the Trust Property being held for such beneficiary to the Estate of said beneficiary.

11. INALIENABILITY OF BENEFICIARY'S INTEREST IN TRUST.

The interest of the Beneficiary(Beneficiaries) under the Trust shall be inalienable. Said Beneficiary(Beneficiaries) can not assign, sell, pledge, encumber or otherwise transfer his(her) inalienable interest in the Trust Property to a third party. Nor can such interest be attached, garnished, levied upon or otherwise subjected to any proceedings whether at law or in equity.

12. BENEFICIARY'S PROPORTIONATE LIABILITY FOR ESTATE TAXES.

Each Beneficiary hereunder shall be liable for his(her) proportionate share of any Estate Taxes that may be levied upon the total value of the Trust Property distributed to said Beneficiaries upon the death of either the Trustor or the survivor of the Trustors.

13. REVOCATION OF DESIGNATION OF BENEFICIARY.

(a) The Trustor(s) are reserved with the right to revoke, at any time, the designation of a herein named Beneficiary, without prior notice to or the consent of any other such Beneficiary.

(b) The Trustor(s) may, at any time, either designate a new beneficiary to replace a previously revoked beneficiary designation or designate an additional beneficiary, notwithstanding all previous beneficiary designations. No prior notice to or the consent of any other beneficiary is required.

(c) In the event any Beneficiary under this Trust shall not survive the Trustor(s), the Trustor(s) may designate a new beneficiary to replace such beneficiary by amending this Declaration of Trust. If however, the Trustor(s) fail(s) to so designate a new beneficiary as herein provided, then, upon the death of either the Trustor or the survivor of the Trustors, such beneficiary's share of the Trust Property shall be distributed in accordance with the survivor designation provided hereinbefore in Paragraph 1.

14. NON-LIABILITY OF THIRD PARTIES.

(a) This Trust is created with the express intent and understanding that any third parties, including their Agents, Employees or Vendors, who, upon the written request of the Trustor(s), or under the color of authority granted to the Trustee(s) in this Trust Instrument, perform any duties or render any services in the furtherance of the purposes and intents of this Trust, absent any showing of fraud, shall be under no liability for the application or proper administration of any assets or properties being the subject of the said third party's acts.

 FORM AT-104 Page 4

FORM AT-105

PAGE 5 OF THE DECLARATION OF TRUST

An example of Page 5 of the TRUST, providing TRUST CLAUSES Numbered 14(b) through 18 and the Notary Acknowledgment.

(b) This limitation of liability gives specific protection to any third party who acts, performs or renders any services pursuant to any Notice, Instrument or Document believed (and represented) to be genuine, and to have been signed and presented by the proper party(parties).

(c) It is further the express intent of this Trust that the non-liability of all Third Parties be given broad and prospective application. In particular, A Despository, Custodial Agent or Financial Institution, including (but not limited to): Banks, Brokerage Firms, Credit Unions, Saving and Loan Associations, Transfer Agents, Thrift Associations, or any other person or entity acting in a Fiduciary capacity with regards to any assets or property comprising the TRUST RES, shall suffer no liability, nor incur any express or implied obiligations when acting in the capacity of a Transferror, upon proper request, of any assets or property either sought to be, or constructively comprising the Trust Res.

15. EXTENSION OF TRUST POWERS.

This DECLARATION OF TRUST shall extend to and be binding upon the Heirs, Executors, Administrators and assigns of the undersigned Trustor(s) and upon the Successor(s) to the Trustee(s).

16. BOND AND EXPENSES.

(a) The Trustee(s) under this DECLARATION OF TRUST shall serve without Bond.

(b) The Successor Trustee may also serve without bond, except that bond *(check one)* ☐ shall (☒ may) be required when, upon the death(s) of the Trustor(s), whichever applicable, the Beneficiary(ies) either shall not have attained majority age or the distribution of the Trust Res to any beneficiary(ies) is limited by a proper document which effectively continues the Trust. The requirement of Bond in this instance shall be in a nominal amount, chargeable to the Trust Res.

(c) The Successor Trustee shall be reimbursed, before final distribution to the Beneficiary(ies), for all out-of-pocket expenses incurred in the discharge of duties as Successor Trustee.

(d) Upon the agreement of the Beneficiary(ies), including the parent(s) or guardian(s) of any such Beneficiary(ies) not of majority age, the Successor Trustee may be reasonably compensated for extraordinary time and efforts employed to accomplish the discharge of duties as Successor Trustee.

17. APPLICABILITY OF STATE LAWS.

This DECLARATION OF TRUST shall be construed and enforced in accordance with the Laws of the State of ____________

(enter here the name of State where Trust will be managed)

18. SAVING CLAUSE.

If a State Court of competent jurisdiction shall at any time invalidate any of the separate provisions of this Declaration of Trust, such invalidation shall not be construed as invalidating the whole of this Declaration of Trust, but only that separate provision in controversy. All of the remaining provisions shall be undisturbed as to their legal force and effect.

IN WITNESS WHEREOF, the Trustor(s) has(have) hereunto set his(her)(their) hand(s) and seal(s) the day and year first above written.

(signature before Notary Public)
(Trustor)

(This section will be completed by Notary Public)

(signature before Notary Public)
(Co-Trustor)

State of ______________________)
) ss. **ACKNOWLEDGMENT**
County of ______________________)

On this _____ day of ______________________, 19 _____, before me, the undersigned Notary Public, personally appeared ____

____,

known to me to be the individual(s) who executed the foregoing instrument and acknowledged the same to be his(her)(their) free act and deed.

My Commission Expires: ______________________ ______________________
Notary Public

 FORM AT-105 Page 5

FORM AT-200a

DEED OF REALTY TO TRUST

An example of the DEED OF REALTY TO TRUST conveying title to the family home to the TRUST.

When recorded, mail to:

Name: JOHN AND SALLY DOE

Address: 123 ANY STREET

City/State/Zip Code: TUCSON, AZ 85700

Space above this line for Recorder's use

DEED OF REALTY TO TRUST

(Conveying Real Property to Trust)

KNOW ALL MEN BY THESE PRESENTS:

That I(we) JOHN LARSEN DOE AND SALLY LOIS DOE, HUSBAND AND WIFE, the undersigned Grantor(s), who is(are) the Trustor(s) under that certain DECLARATION OF TRUST, known as (and hereafter referred to as) DOE FAMILY TRUST NO. D-1, dated FEBRUARY 1ST, 19 92, do by these presents, hereby convey IN TRUST [(*check box if applicable*) ☒ as Trust Property No. 2] unto JOHN LARSEN DOE AND SALLY LOIS DOE, as Trustee(s) under said Trust, all of my(our) rights, title and interest in and to that certain parcel of real property situated in PIMA County, State of ARIZONA, and described as: LOT 24, BLOCK 30 OF TUCSON VALLEY ESTATE, ACCORDING TO THE PLATS OF RECORD IN THE OFFICE OF THE PIMA COUNTY RECORDER, STATE OF ARIZONA, IN BOOK 378 OF MAPS AND PLATS AT PAGES 37-43.

The Grantor(s) asserts an interest in the aforesaid property pursuant to an instrument conveying title to real property dated APRIL 4TH, 19 42, and recorded in the Official Land Records of PIMA County, State of ARIZONA, in Docket(Book)(Volume) 4442 at page(s) 161.

TO HAVE AND TO HOLD the said premises unto and to the use of the said Trustee(s) and his(her)(their) successors in interest forever; and that neither I(we) nor my(our) heirs or assigns shall have nor make any claims or demands upon said property.

IN WITNESS WHEREOF, I(we) have hereunto set my(our) hand(s) and seal this 1ST day of FEBRUARY 19 92.

Witness (only if required under State Laws) — John Larsen Doe — Grantor/Trustor

Witness (only if required under State Laws) — Sally Lois Doe — Co-Grantor/Co-Trustor

FORM AT-200a Page 1

FORM AT-201a
QUIT CLAIM DEED TO TRUST

An example of the QUIT CLAIM DEED TO TRUST quitclaiming a realty interest to the TRUST.

When recorded, mail to:

Name: JOHN AND SALLY DOE

Address: 123 ANY STREET

City/State/Zip Code: TUCSON, AZ 85700

Space above this line for Recorder's use

QUIT CLAIM DEED TO TRUST
(Releasing Real Estate Contract Interest to Trust)

KNOW ALL MEN BY THESE PRESENTS:

That I(we) JOHN LARSEN DOE AND SALLY LOIS DOE, HUSBAND AND WIFE, the undersigned Releasor(s), who is(are) the Trustor(s) under that certain DECLARATION OF TRUST, known as (and hereafter referred to as) DOE FAMILY TRUST NO. D-1, dated FEBRUARY 1ST, 19 92, do by these presents, hereby release, remise and forever Quit Claim IN TRUST [(*check box if applicable*) ☒ as Trust Property No. 1] unto JOHN LARSEN DOE AND SALLY LOIS DOE, as Trustee(s) under said Trust, all of my(our) rights, title and interest in and to that certain Property situated in DENVER County, State of COLORADO, and described as: LOT 2, BLOCK 4, CHERRY MOUNTAIN SUBDIVISION, ACCORDING TO THE PLAT OF RECORD IN THE OFFICE OF THE DENVER COUNTY RECORDER, STATE OF COLORADO, IN BOOK 4889 OF MAPS AND PLATS AT PAGES 382-400.

The Releasor(s) asserts an interest in the aforesaid property pursuant to an agreement(contract) to acquire said property dated SEPTEMBER 25, 19 88, which said agreement(contract) is recorded in the Official Land Records of DENVER County, State of COLORADO, in Docket(Book)(Volume) 9861 at page(s) 142-143.

TO HAVE AND TO HOLD the said interest in the above described property unto and to the use of the said Trustee(s) and his(her)(their) successors in interest forever; and that neither I(we) nor my(our) heirs or assigns shall have nor make any claims or demands upon said property interest.

IN WITNESS WHEREOF, I(we) have hereunto set my(our) hand(s) and seal this 1ST day of FEBRUARY 19 92.

Witness (only if required under State Laws) — *John Larsen Doe* Releasor/Trustor

Witness (only if required under State Laws) — *Jane Lois Doe* Co-Releasor/Co-Trustor

FORM AT-202

FINANCIAL ACCOUNT TRANSFER TO TRUST

An example of the transfer to the TRUST of 3 separate Bank Accounts at the same Bank.

FINANCIAL ACCOUNT TRANSFER TO TRUST

(☒ Financial Institution ☐ Brokerage Firm)

To: MOUNTAIN NATIONAL BANK
1010 ASH STREET
TUCSON, AZ 85700

KNOW ALL MEN BY THESE PRESENTS:

That I (we) JOHN LARSEN DOE AND SALLY LOIS DOE, the undersigned Transferor(s), who is(are) the Trustor(s) under that certain DECLARATION OF TRUST, known as (and hereafter referred to as) DOE FAMILY TRSUT NO. D-1 , dated FEBRUARY 1, 19 92, do by these presents, hereby assign, transfer and set over IN TRUST [(*check box if applicable*) ☒ as Trust Property No. 2] unto JOHN LARSEN DOE AND SALLY LOIS DOE, as Trustee(s) under said TRUST, all of my(our) rights, title and interest in and to (check one):

☒ Financial Account No(s): 238-2829; 431-8338 AND 345-2929 ;
☐ Brokerage Account No(s): ;
at the Financial Institution or Firm known as: MOUNTAIN NATIONAL BANK

whose address is: 1010 ASH STREET, TUCSON, AZ 85700 ,

including all cash and/or securities held in said Account.

Said account(s) or Securities shall hereafter be owned by, designated and entitled, as follows: JOHN LARSEN DOE AND SALLY LOIS DOE, TRUSTEES UNDER DOE FAMILY TRUST NO. D-1 .

TO HAVE AND TO HOLD the said Account(s), including all cash and/or Securities held therein, unto and to the use and benefit of the said Trustee(s) and his(her)(their) Successors in interest forever; and that neither I(we) nor my(our) heirs or assigns have nor make any claims or demands upon said Financial Account Interest.

IN WITNESS WHEREOF, I(We) have signed these presents this 1ST day of FEBRUARY , 19 92

John Larsen Doe
Transferor/Trustor

Sally Lois Doe
Co-Transferor/Co-Trustor

State of ARIZONA)
) ss.
County of PIMA)

ACKNOWLEDGMENT

On this 1ST day of FEBRUARY , 19 92, before me, the undersigned Notary Public, personally appeared, JOHN LARSEN DOE AND SALLY LOIS DOE , to me known to be the individual(s) described in and who executed the foregoing instrument and acknowledged that he(she)(they) executed the same for the purposes therein contained.

My Commission Expires: MARCH 4, 1992

Frank O Lous
Notary Public

 FORM AT-202

FORM AT-202

FINANCIAL ACCOUNT TRANSFER TO TRUST

An example of the transfer to the TRUST of a Stock Brokerage Account.

FINANCIAL ACCOUNT TRANSFER TO TRUST

(☐ Financial Institution ☒ Brokerage Firm)

To: MERRILL, STREET AND COMPANY
1306 COLFAX STREET
DENVER, CO 79000

KNOW ALL MEN BY THESE PRESENTS:

That I (we) JOHN LARSEN DOE AND SALLY LOIS DOE, the undersigned Transferor(s), who is(are) the Trustor(s) under that certain DECLARATION OF TRUST, known as (and hereafter referred to as) DOE FAMILY TRUST NO. D-1, dated FEBRUARY 1, 19 92, do by these presents, hereby assign, transfer and set over IN TRUST [(*check box if applicable*) ☒ as Trust Property No. 1] unto JOHN LARSEN DOE AND SALLY LOIS DOE, as Trustee(s) under said TRUST, all of my(our) rights, title and interest in and to (check one):

☐ Financial Account No(s): ______;

☒ Brokerage Account No(s): MC128743;

at the Financial Institution or Firm known as: MERRIL, STREET AND COMPANY

whose address is: 1306 COLFAX STREET, DENVER, CO 79000,

including all cash and/or securities held in said Account.

Said account(s) or Securities shall hereafter be owned by, designated and entitled, as follows: JOHN LARSEN DOE AND SALLY LOIS DOE, TRUSTEES UNDER DOE FAMILY TRUST NO. D-1.

TO HAVE AND TO HOLD the said Account(s), including all cash and/or Securities held therein, unto and to the use and benefit of the said Trustee(s) and his(her)(their) Successors in interest forever; and that neither I(we) nor my(our) heirs or assigns have nor make any claims or demands upon said Financial Account Interest.

IN WITNESS WHEREOF, I(We) have signed these presents this 3RD day of FEBRUARY, 19 92

John Larsen Doe
Transferor/Trustor

Sally Lois Doe
Co-Transferor/Co-Trustor

State of ARIZONA)
) ss.
County of PIMA)

ACKNOWLEDGMENT

On this 3RD day of FEBRUARY, 19 92, before me, the undersigned Notary Public, personally appeared, JOHN LARSEN DOE AND SALLY LOIS DOE, to me known to be the individual(s) described in and who executed the foregoing instrument and acknowledged that he(she)(they) executed the same for the purposes therein contained.

My Commission Expires: MARCH 4, 1995

Frank O Louis
Notary Public

FORM AT-202

FORM AT-203

SECURITIES TRANSFER TO TRUST

An example of the transfer to TRUST of 5,000 Shares of Common Stock of Standard Oil Of California.

SECURITIES TRANSFER TO TRUST

(☒ Stocks ☐ Bonds ☐ Other)

To: CENTRAL BANK & TRUST CO.
1111 BROADWAY PLAZA
NEW YORK, NY 10020

KNOW ALL MEN BY THESE PRESENTS:

That I (we) JOHN LARSEN DOE AND SALLY LOIS DOE,
the undersigned Transferor(s), who is(are) the Trustor(s) under that certain DECLARATION OF TRUST, known as (and hereafter referred to as) DOE FAMILY TRUST NO. D-1,
dated FEBRUARY 1, 19 92, by these presents, does(do) hereby assign, transfer and deliver IN TRUST [(*check box if applicable*) ☒ as Trust Property No. 3] unto JOHN LARSEN DOE AND SALLY LOIS DOE,
as Trustee(s) under said TRUST, all of my(our) rights, title and interest in and to the securities described as:
5,000 SHARES OF COMMON STOCK OF STANDARD OIL OF CALIFORNIA;
standing in the name of the undersigned on the books of said Company.

Said Securities shall hereafter be owned by, designated and entitled on the books of said Company, as follows:
JOHN LARSEN DOE AND SALLY LOUIS DOE, TRUSTEES UNDER DOE FAMILY TRUST NO. D-1.

TO HAVE AND TO HOLD the said securities unto and to the use of said Trustee and his(her)(their) successors in interest forever; and that neither I(we) nor my(our) heirs or assigns shall have nor make any claim or demand upon such securities.

IN WITNESS WHEREOF, I(we) have signed these presents this 1ST day of FEBRUARY, 19 92.

John Larsen Doe
Transferor/Trustor

Sally Lois Doe
Co-Transferor/Co-Trustor

PLEASE NOTE:
The signature of the Transferor(s) must be guaranteed by an officer of a commercial bank, trust company, or by a member of the New York Stock Exchange or another national securities exchange where transferor(s) has(have) an active account or signature on file. Notarized or witnessed signatures are not acceptable for securities transfers.

(Affix Signature Guaranteed Stamp Below)

(SIGNATURE GUARANTEED STAMP OF MOUNTAIN NATIONAL BANK, TUCSON, ARIZONA)

FORM AT-203

FORM AT-203

SECURITIES TRANSFER TO TRUST

An example of the transfer to TRUST of a Registered Limited Partnership Certificate.

SECURITIES TRANSFER TO TRUST

(☐ Stocks ☐ Bonds ☒ Other)

To: VALLEY MANAGEMENT ASSOCIATES
440 BAYSIDE LANE
SAN FRANCISCO, CA 92000

KNOW ALL MEN BY THESE PRESENTS:

That I (we) JOHN LARSEN DOE AND SALLY LOIS DOE, the undersigned Transferor(s), who is(are) the Trustor(s) under that certain DECLARATION OF TRUST, known as (and hereafter referred to as) DOE FAMILY TRUST NO. D-1, dated FEBRUARY 1, 19 92, by these presents, does(do) hereby assign, transfer and deliver IN TRUST [(*check box if applicable*) ☒ as Trust Property No. 3] unto JOHN LARSEN DOE AND SALLY LOIS DOE, as Trustee(s) under said TRUST, all of my(our) rights, title and interest in and to the securities described as: A REGISTERED LIMITED PARTNERSHIP INTEREST IN VALLEY FINANCIAL GROUP, CERTIFICATE NO. K-43200; standing in the name of the undersigned on the books of said Company.

Said Securities shall hereafter be owned by, designated and entitled on the books of said Company, as follows: JOHN LARSEN DOE AND SALLY LOIS DOE, TRUSTEES UNDER DOE FAMILY TRUST NO. D-1.

TO HAVE AND TO HOLD the said securities unto and to the use of said Trustee and his(her)(their) successors in interest forever; and that neither I(we) nor my(our) heirs or assigns shall have nor make any claim or demand upon such securities.

IN WITNESS WHEREOF, I(we) have signed these presents this 1ST day of FEBRUARY, 19 92.

John Larsen Doe
Transferor/Trustor

Sally Lois Doe
Co-Transferor/Co-Trustor

PLEASE NOTE:
The signature of the Transferor(s) must be guaranteed by an officer of a commercial bank, trust company, or by a member of the New York Stock Exchange or another national securities exchange where transferor(s) has(have) an active account or signature on file. Notarized or witnessed signatures are not acceptable for securities transfers.

(Affix Signature Guaranteed Stamp Below)

(SIGNATURE GUARANTEED STAMP OF MOUNTAIN NATIONAL BANK, TUCSON, ARIZONA)

 FORM AT-203

FORM AT-204a

ASSIGNMENT OF SECURED REALTY INTEREST TO TRUST

An example of the assignment to the TRUST of a Beneficial Interest in a Deed Of Trust.

When recorded, mail to:

Name: JOHN AND SALLY DOE

Address: 123 ANY STREET

City/State/Zip Code: TUCSON, AZ 85700

Space above this line for Recorder's use

ASSIGNMENT OF SECURED REALTY INTEREST TO TRUST

(☒ Deed Of Trust ☐ Realty Mortgage)

KNOW ALL MEN BY THESE PRESENTS:

That I (we) JOHN LARSEN DOE AND SALLY LOIS DOE, the undersigned Assignor(s), who is(are) the Trustor(s) under that certain DECLARATION OF TRUST, known as (and hereafter referred to as) DOE FAMILY TRUST NO. D-1, dated FEBRUARY 1, 19 92, do by these presents, hereby assign, transfer and set over IN TRUST [(*check box if applicable*) ☒ as Trust Property No. 3] unto JOHN LARSEN DOE AND SALLY LOIS DOE, as Trustee(s) under said Trust, all of my(our) rights, title and interest in and to that certain:

(check one)

☒ Beneficial Interest In Deed Of Trust ☐ Realty Mortgage

and to the Note or other evidence of indebtedness secured thereby, dated APRIL 18, 19 89, and recorded in the Official Land Records of PIMA County, State of ARIZONA, in Docket(Book)(Volume) 5066, at page(s) ________.

TO HAVE AND TO HOLD the said Security Interest, including all benefits payable thereunder, unto and to the use of the said Trustee(s) and his(her)(their) successors in interest forever; and that neither I(we) nor my(our) heirs or assigns shall have nor make any claims or demands upon said Secured Realty Interest.

IN WITNESS WHEREOF, I(we) have hereunto set my(our) hand(s) and seal this 1ST day of FEBRUARY 19 92.

____
Witness (Only if required under State law)

John Larsen Doe
Assignor/Trustor

____
Witness (Only if required under State law)

Sally Lois Doe
Co-Assignor/Co-Trustor

FORM AT-205a

CHATTEL TRANSFER TO TRUST

An example of the transfer to TRUST of household furnishings, appliances, exercise equipment, photographs, portraits, kitchenware, dishes and window and bed coverings.

When recorded, mail to:

Name: JOHN AND SALLY DOE

Address: 123 ANY STREET

City/State/Zip Code: TUCSON, AZ 85700

Space above this line for Recorder's use

CHATTEL TRANSFER TO TRUST

(Transferring Personal Property to Trust)

KNOW ALL MEN BY THESE PRESENTS:

That I (we) JOHN LARSEN DOE AND SALLY LOIS DOE, the undersigned Transferors(s), who is(are) the Trustor(s) under that certain DECLARATION OF TRUST, known as (and hereafter referred to as) DOE FAMILY TRUST NO. D-1, dated FEBRUARY 1, 19 92, do by these presents, hereby assign, transfer and deliver IN TRUST [(*check box if applicable)* ☐ as Trust Property No. 2] unto JOHN LARSEN DOE AND SALLY LOIS DOE, as Trustee(s) under said Trust, all of my(our) rights, title and interest in and to the following Chattel Property, to wit: ALL HOUSHOLD FURNISHING, APPLIANCES AND EFFECTS IN THE FAMILY HOME LOCATED AT 123 ANY STREET, TUCSON, ARIZONA, WHICH INCLUDES: 5 ROOMS OF FURNITURE, REFRIGERATOR, WASHER AND DRYER, EXERCISE EQUIPMENT, PHOTOGRAPHS AND PORTRAITS, KITCHEN WARE AND DISHES, AND ALL WINDOW AND BED COVERINGS.

Said Chattel Property shall hereafter be owned by, designated and entitled, as follows: JOHN LARSEN DOE AND SALLY LOIS DOE, TRUSTEES UNDER DOE FAMILY TRUST NO. D-1.

TO HAVE AND TO HOLD all of the said Chattel Property unto and to the use of the said Trustee(s) and his(her)(their) successors in interest forever; and I(we) do hereby covenant to and with the said Trustee(s) and his(her)(their) successors in interest; that I(we) am(are) the legal owner(s) of the said Chattel Property; that it is free and clear of any claims, encumbrances or liens; that I(we) have the absolute right to assign, transfer and deliver said Chattel Property as aforesaid; that I(we) am(are) in peaceable possession of said Chattel Property; and that I(we) will forever warrant and defend the same against the lawful claims and demands of all persons whomsoever.

IN WITNESS WHEREOF, I(we) have hereunto set my(our) hand(s) and seal this 1ST day of FEBRUARY 19 92.

John Larsen Doe
Transferor/Trustor

Sally Lois Doe
Co-Transferor/Co-Trustor

 FORM AT-205a **Page 1**

FORM AT-205a

CHATTEL TRANSFER TO TRUST

An example of the transfer to TRUST of a 1990 Buick Automobile.

When recorded, mail to:

Name: JOHN AND SALLY DOE

Address: 123 ANY STREET

City/State/Zip Code: TUCSON, AZ 85700

Space above this line for Recorder's use

CHATTEL TRANSFER TO TRUST

(Transferring Personal Property to Trust)

KNOW ALL MEN BY THESE PRESENTS:

That I (we) JOHN LARSEN DOE AND SALLY LOIS DOE, the undersigned Transferors(s), who is(are) the Trustor(s) under that certain DECLARATION OF TRUST, known as (and hereafter referred to as) DOE FAMILY TRUST NO. D-1, dated FEBRUARY 1, 19 92, do by these presents, hereby assign, transfer and deliver IN TRUST [(*check box if applicable)* ☒ as Trust Property No. 2] unto JOHN LARSEN DOE AND SALLY LOIS DOE, as Trustee(s) under said Trust, all of my(our) rights, title and interest in and to the following Chattel Property, to wit: 1990 BUICK REGAL, SERIAL NO. GMC0374123NO15.

Said Chattel Property shall hereafter be owned by, designated and entitled, as follows: JOHN LARSEN DOE AND SALLY LOIS DOE, TRUSTEES UNDER DOE FAMILY TRUST NO. D-1

TO HAVE AND TO HOLD all of the said Chattel Property unto and to the use of the said Trustee(s) and his(her)(their) successors in interest forever; and I(we) do hereby covenant to and with the said Trustee(s) and his(her)(their) successors in interest; that I(we) am(are) the legal owner(s) of the said Chattel Property; that it is free and clear of any claims, encumbrances or liens; that I(we) have the absolute right to assign, transfer and deliver said Chattel Property as aforesaid; that I(we) am(are) in peaceable possession of said Chattel Property; and that I(we) will forever warrant and defend the same against the lawful claims and demands of all persons whomsoever.

IN WITNESS WHEREOF, I(we) have hereunto set my(our) hand(s) and seal this 1ST day of FEBRUARY 19 92.

John Larsen Doe
Transferor/Trustor

Sally Lois Doe
Co-Transferor/Co-Trustor

 FORM AT-205a **Page 1**

FORM AT-206

ASSIGNMENT OF CONTRACT TO TRUST

An example of the transfer to TRUST of a Royalty Contract.

ASSIGNMENT OF CONTRACT TO TRUST

(Non-Realty Contract)

To: ALAMO INDUSTRAIL SUPPLIES INC.
5748 S. HIGHWAY 389
FORT WAYNE, IN 46800

KNOW ALL MEN BY THESE PRESENTS:

That I (we) JOHN LARSEN DOE, the undersigned Assignor(s), who is(are) the Trustor(s) under that certain DECLARATION OF TRUST known as (and hereafter referred to as) DOE FAMILY TRUST NO. D-1, dated FEBRUARY 1, 19 92, do by these Presents, hereby assign, transfer and set over IN TRUST [(*check box if applicable*) ☒ as Trust Property No. 1] unto JOHN LARSEN DOE AND SALLY LOIS DOE, as Trustee(s) under said TRUST, all of my (our) rights, title and interest in and to that certain contract, dated JULY 22, 19 83, executed by ALAMO INDUSTRIAL SUPPLIES, INC., in favor of JOHN LARSEN DOE, under the terms of which certain payments accrue to me(us) by virtue of MY ASSIGNMENT OF INTEREST AS REGISTRANT UNDER THAT CERTAIN DESIGN PATENT NUMBERED 170301, AND SUBSEQUENT PATENT ROUALTY CONTRACT EXECUTED BY AFORESAID ALAMO INDUSTRIAL SUPPLIES, INC., IN FAVOR OF JOHN LARSEN DOE.

Said Contract shall hereafter be owned by, designated and entitled, as follows: JOHN LARSEN DOE AND SALLY LOIS DOE, TRUSTEES UNDER DOE FAMILY TRUST NO. D-1.

TO HAVE AND TO HOLD the said Contract Interest unto and to the use of the said Trustee(s) and Successor(s) in interest forever, and that neither I(we) nor my(our) heirs or assigns shall have nor make any claim or demand upon such contract interest.

IN WITNESS WHEREOF, I(we) have signed these presents this 1ST day of FEBRUARY, 19 92.

John Larsen Doe
Assignor/Trustor

Co-Assignor/Co-Trustor

State of ARIZONA)
) ss.
County of PIMA)

ACKNOWLEDGMENT

On this 1ST day of FEBRUARY, 19 92, before me, the undersigned Notary Public, personally appeared, JOHN LARSEN DOE, to me known to be the individual(s) described in and who executed the foregoing instrument and acknowledged that he(she)(they) executed the same for the purposes therein contained.

My Commission Expires: MARCH 4, 1995

Frank O. Lowry
Notary Public

FORM AT-206

FORM AT-207a

BUSINESS INTEREST TRANSFER TO TRUST

An example of the transfer to TRUST of a sole proprietorship business interest known as Doe Computer Sales and Service.

When recorded, mail to:

Name: JOHN AND SALLY DOE

Address: 123 ANY STREET

City/State/Zip Code: TUCSON, AZ 85700

Space above this line for Recorder's use

BUSINESS INTEREST TRANSFER TO TRUST

(☒ Sole Proprietorship ☐ Partnership)

KNOW ALL MEN BY THESE PRESENTS:

That I (we) JOHN LARSEN DOE, the undersigned Transferor(s), who is(are) the Trustor(s) under that certain DECLARATION OF TRUST, known as (and hereafter referred to as) DOE FAMILY TRUST NO. D-1, dated FEBRUARY 1, 19 92, do by these presents, hereby assign, transfer and set over IN TRUST [(*check box if applicable*) ☒ as Trust Property No. 3] unto JOHN LARSEN DOE AND SALLY LOIS DOE, as Trustee(s) under said Trust, all of my(our) rights, title and interest in and to that certain Business Organization known, as: DOE COMPUTER SALES AND SERVICE, and located at: 1099 COMPUTER LANE, SAN DIEGO, CALIFORNIA, which is a (check one)

☒ Sole Proprietorship (☐ Partnership with general partners ____ and ____; my(our) interest in said partnership being ____ percent).

Said Business Interest shall be hereafter owned by, designated and entitled, as follows: JOHN LARSEN DOE AND SALLY LARSEN DOE, TRUSTEES UNDER DOE FAMILY TRUST NO. D-1, DOING BUSINESS AS, DOE COMPUTER SALES AND SERVICE.

TO HAVE AND TO HOLD the said Business Interest unto and to the use of the said Trustee(s) and his(her)(their) Successors in Interest forever; and that neither I(we) nor my(our) heirs or assigns shall have nor make any claims or demands upon said Business Interest.

IN WITNESS WHEREOF, I(we) have signed these presents this 1ST day of FEBRUARY, 19 92.

John Larsen Doe
Transferor/Trustor

Co-Transferor/Co-Trustor

FORM AT-300

NOTICE OF TRUST

An example of a NOTICE OF TRUST with Husband and Wife Trustors. This notice is required in some States. See foot note at bottom of form.

NOTICE OF TRUST*

(Revocable Trust)

To: CLERK OF THE CIRCUIT COURT
PROBATE DIVISION
Name of Court

P.O. BOX 1110
Address

TAMPA, FL 33601
City/State/Zip Code

PLEASE TAKE NOTICE:

Pursuant to the applicable provisions of the Uniform Probate Code, Notice is hereby given that a REVOCABLE TRUST, known as (and hereafter referred to as) DOE FAMILY TRUST NO. D-1 was established the 1ST day of FEBRUARY, 19 92, in the jurisdiction of this Court, by and between the Trustor(s) and Trustee(s) below named:

TRUSTOR(S):

(1) JOHN LARSEN DOE
Name
123 ANY STREET
Address
TAMPA, FL 32000
City/State/Zip

(2) SALLY LOIS DOE
Name
123 ANY STREET
Address
TAMPA, FL 32000
City/State/Zip

TRUSTEE(S):

(3) JOHN LARSEN DOE
Name
123 ANY STREET
Address
TAMPA, FL 32000
City/State/Zip

(4) SALLY LOIS DOE
Name
123 ANY STREET
Address
TAMPA, FL 32000
City/State/Zip

Dated this 5TH day of FEBRUARY, 19 92.

John Larsen Doe
Trustor

Sally Lois Doe
Co-Trustor

State of FLORIDA)
) ss.
County of HILLSBORO)

ACKNOWLEDGMENT

On this 5TH day of FEBRUARY, 19 92, before me, the undersigned Notary Public, personally appeared, JOHN LARSEN DOE AND SALLY LOIS DOE ________, to me known to be the individual(s) described in and who executed the foregoing instrument and acknowledged that he(she)(they) executed the same as his(her)(their) free act and deed.

My Commission Expires: mARCH 4, 1995

Frank O Louis
Notary Public

***PLEASE NOTE:** This NOTICE OF TRUST is only required if the State where you plan to establish the LIVING TRUST has provisions for filing this NOTICE with a Court of Jurisdiction; for example, the Probate Court. Many States do not have provisions for filing this NOTICE (you must call the Court and ask), therefore, if the Court does not require this NOTICE, then simply disregard it.

FORM AT-300

FORM AT-400a

PAGE 1 OF THE LAST WILL AND TESTAMENT

An example of Page 1 of the LAST WILL AND TESTAMENT of the husband. This Page 1 is the front of the form, Page 2 is on the back.

THE LAST WILL AND TESTAMENT
of
JOHN LARSEN DOE

I, JOHN LARSEN DOE,
also known as J. LARSEN DOE,
a resident of the STATE of ARIZONA,
which I do declare to be my place of domicile, being of sound and disposing mind and memory, do hereby make, publish and declare this to be my Last Will and Testament, thus revoking all Wills and Codicils to Wills previously made by me.

FIRST (Debt Clause): I direct that the Executor(Executrix) hereinafter named pursuant to this Last Will and Testament, pay (as soon after my death as practical) all of my just debts and obligations, including funeral expenses and the expenses incident to my last illness, but excepting those long term debts secured by real or personal property which may be assumed by the person designated to receive such property.

SECOND (Distribution Clause): I give, devise and bequeath all of the rest, remainder and residue of my estate, whether real or personal property of whatsoever kind or character, and wherever situated, to the Successor Trustee named and appointed by me under that certain Declaration Of Trust, known as DOE FAMILY TRUST NO. D-1, dated FEBRUARY 1, 19 92, as then written or thereafter amended, to be added to the property then held IN TRUST and become one and a part of the Trust Corpus, subject to the terms and conditions of said Declaration Of Trust, except the following property, if any, which shall be given as follows:

TO MY GRANDSON, WALTER J. ROE, I GIVE MY ENTIRE COIN AND STAMP COLLECTION.

THIRD (Common Disaster Clause): If my spouse, if any, shall die as a result of a common disaster with me, then my spouse shall be deemed to have (check one): ☒ survived me (☐ predeceased me).

FOURTH (Survivorship Clause): If any person(s) named in this Last Will and Testament, other than my spouse, shall not survive me, then that share of my estate which would have been distributed to such person(s) had he(she)(they) survived me, shall be distributed (*check one*): ☒ per stirpes (☐ per capita).

FIFTH (Executor(Executrix) Appointment Clause): I hereby nominate, constitute and appoint as the Executor (Executrix) of my Estate: SALLY LOIS DOE,
provided, however, that in the event he(she) is unable or unwilling to so serve in such capacity, then I nominate, constitute and appoint FRANKLIN G. DOE.

SIXTH (Guardian Appointment Clause): I hereby nominate, constitute and appoint as the Guardian of any minor child(ren) of mine: SALLY LOIS DOE,
provided, however, that in the event he(she) is unable or unwilling to so serve in that capacity, then I nominate, constitute and appoint DOROTHY A ROE.

SEVENTH (Saving Clause): In the event any separate provision of this Last Will and Testament is held to be invalid by a Court of competent jurisdiction, then such finding shall not invalidate this entire Last Will and Testament, but only the subject provision.

IN WITNESS WHEREOF, I have hereunto signed this, my Last Will and Testament, this 5TH day of FEBRUARY, 19 92, in the CITY of TUCSON,
State of ARIZONA.

John Larsen Doe
Testator(Testatrix)

 FORM AT-400a Page 1

FORM AT-400b

PAGE 2 OF THE LAST WILL AND TESTAMENT

An example of Page 2 of the LAST WILL AND TESTAMENT of the husband. This Page 2 is on the back of Page 1.

ATTESTATION CLAUSE

The foregoing Last Will and Testament was on the above date, subscribed, sealed, published and declared by the Testator(Testatrix), above named, as his(her) Last Will and Testament in the presence of each of us below named Witnesses, and at the same time, we at his(her) request in his(her) presence and in the presence of each other who hereunto subscribed our names as witnesses hereto; this Attestation Clause having been first read aloud and we hereby certify that at the time of the execution hereof, we believe the Testator(Testatrix) to be of sound and disposing mind and memory.

Marth Lieb of 4460 TOWN PLACE
Address
TUCSON, ARIZONA
City State

Harold Duran of 13602 GOLF LANE
Address
TUCSON, ARZOPMA
City State

______ of ______
Address
______
City State

AFFIDAVIT TO SELF-PROVE LAST WILL AND TESTAMENT[1]

State of ARIZONA)
) ss.
County of PIMA)

WE, MARTHA LIEB, ______,
and HAROLD DURAN, the witnesses whose names are signed to the attached or foregoing instrument, being first duly sworn, do hereby declare to the undersigned authority that the testator(testatrix) signed and executed the foregoing instrument as his(her) Last Will and Testament, that he(she) had signed willingly (or willingly directed another to sign for him(her), that he(she) executed it as his(her) free and voluntary act for the purposes therein expressed; that each of the witnesses, in the presence of each other and hearing of the testator(testatrix), signed the Last Will and Testament as witnesses; and that to the best of their knowledge, the testator(testatrix) was at that time eighteen years of age or older, of sound mind and under no constraint or undue influence.

Martha Lieb
Witness Signature

Harold Duran
Witness Signature

______
Witness Signature

SUBSCRIBED AND SWORN to before me this 5TH day of FEBRUARY, 19 92.

My Commission expires: DECEMBER 1, 1994

Joe Notary
Notary Public

Note 1. This Affidavit merely self-proves the Last Will and Testament in the event all of the Witnesses are unavailable when this Will is probated. It is not, therefore, required to validate this Will, but only an option (see Note 2.).

Note 2. This Last Will and Testament is a witnessed Will which means it will not be valid unless it is witnessed (signed) by the number of witnesses required under State Laws who do not have an interest in the estate of the person making this Last Will and Testament. (*See: Witness Requirements*, Page 11 of Instruction Guide)

FORM AT-500
DISCLAIMER BY SPOUSE

An example of a disclaimer of interest in certain property by a wife who is not a Trustor under the Trust.

When recorded, mail to:

Name: JOHN LARSEN DOE

Address: 123 ANY STREET

City/State/Zip Code: TUCSON, AZ 85700

Space above this line for Recorder's use

DISCLAIMER BY SPOUSE

This DISCLAIMER BY SPOUSE, executed this 1ST day of FEBRUARY, 19 92, by SALLY LOIS DOE, the undersigned (check one) ☐Husband (☒ Wife) of JOHN LARSEN DOE, hereinafter referred to as the "spouse"; Whereas:

1. The spouse is the Trustor under that certain DECLARATION OF TRUST known as (and hereafter referred to as) TRUST NO. D-1, dated FEBRUARY 1ST, 19 92;

2. The spouse has heretofore acquired certain property either with his(her) separate funds or by gift or bequest; said property being situated in PIMA County, State of ARIZONA, and described as: LOT 24, BLOCK 30 OF TUCSON VALLEY ESTATE, ACCORDING TO THE PLATS OF RECORD IN THE OFFICE OF THE PIMA COUNTY RECORDER, STATE OF ARIZONA, IN BOOK 378 OF MAPS AND PLATS AT PAGES 37-43.

3. The undersigned has no past or present claim, interest. lien, rights or title in and to the above described property;

4. The undersigned waives all community property rights, curtesy or dower rights and/or any other rights to said property which may be accorded to me under applicable State Laws, if any.

NOW THEREFORE, in consideration of the premises, the undersigned does hereby disclaim, remise, release and quit claim unto the aforesaid Spouse, his(her) heirs and assignees forever, all rights, title, interest, claim or demands which the undersigned might have, or appear to have under law, in and to the above described property.

IN WITNESS WHEREOF, I have signed this DISCLAIMER BY SPOUSE, the year and date first above written.

______________________ Witness(if required under State Laws)

(WIFE'S SIGNATURE BEFORE NOTARY) Signature of Disclaiming Spouse

______________________ Witness(if required under State Laws)

(TO BE COMPLETED BY NOTARY PUBLIC)

ACKNOWLEDGMENT

State of ______________)
) ss.
County of ______________)

On this ______ day of ______________, 19 ____, before me, the undersigned Notary Public, personally appeared, ______________________, to me known to be the individual described in and who executed the foregoing Instrument and acknowledged that he(she) executed the same for the purposes therein contained.

My Commission Expires: ______________ ______________ Notary Public

 FORM AT-500

FORM AT-600

AMENDMENT TO TRUST ENLARGING POWERS OF TRUSTEE(S)

An example of the TRUST AMENDMENT giving the Trustee the right and authority to deal in commodity and currency contracts.

AMENDMENT TO TRUST
ENLARGING POWERS OF TRUSTEE(S)

To: MERRILL, STREET AND COMPANY
1306 COLFAX STREET
DENVER, CO 79000

KNOW ALL MEN BY THESE PRESENTS:

That I(we) JOHN LARSEN DOE AND SALLY LOIS DOE, the undersigned Trustor(s) under that certain DECLARATION OF TRUST known as (and hereafter referred to as) DOE FAMILY TRUST NO. D-1, dated FEBRUARY 1, 19 92; and pursuant to the applicable provisions of said TRUST, do by these presents, hereby amend said TRUST to clarify, define, enlarge, modify, or otherwise grant to Trustee(s) unrestricted authority and power under Paragraph 6(a) of said TRUST, to BUY, TRADE OR OTHERWISE DEAL IN ALL TYPES OF COMMODITY AND CURRENCY CONTRACTS IN THE NAME OF THE DOE FAMILY TRUST NO. D-1.

WHEREAS, under Paragraph 3(a) of said TRUST, the Trustor(s) has(have) the authority, right and power to amend or modify said Trust.

NOW THEREFORE, pursuant to such authority, right and power to amend said TRUST, the Trustor(s) hereby elect to amend Paragraph 6(a), Powers of the Trustee(s), to include those powers herein described.

IN WITNESS WHEREOF, I(we) have signed these presents this 1ST day of APRIL, 19 92.

John Larsen Doe
Trustor

Sally Lois Doe
Co-Trustor

State of ARIZONA)
) ss
County of PIMA)

ACKNOWLEDGMENT

On this 1ST day of APRIL, 19 92, before me, the undersigned Notary Public, personally appeared, JOHN LARSEN DOE AND SALLY LOIS DOE, to me known to be the individual(s) described in and who executed the foregoing Instrument and acknowledged that he(she)(they) executed the same for the purposes therein contained.

My Commission Expires: MARCH 4, 1995

Frank O Louis
Notary Public

FORM AT-600

FORM AT-601a

AMENDMENT TO TRUST LIMITING DISTRIBUTION OF ASSETS TO A BENEFICIARY

An example of the TRUST AMENDMENT limiting a Beneficiary to quarterly payments when the Trust Property is ultimately distributed.

AMENDMENT TO TRUST LIMITING DISTRIBUTION OF ASSETS TO A BENEFICIARY

KNOW ALL MEN BY THESE PRESENTS:

That I(we) JOHN LARSEN DOE AND SALLY LOIS DOE, the undersigned Trustor(s), under that certain DECLARATION OF TRUST known as (and hereafter referred to as) DOE FAMILY TRUST NO. D-1, dated FEBRUARY 1, 19 92, and pursuant to Paragraph 3(a) of said Trust, do by these presents hereby amend and modify Paragraph 11(a) of said Trust to enlarge the power of the Successor Trustee(s) to continue IN TRUST that share of the Trust assets which are determined to be distributable to Trust Beneficiary FRANKLIN G. DOE and pay or disburse the same to said Beneficiary in (check one) ☐ Monthly (☒ Quarterly) (☐ Annual) payments not exceeding $ 900.00, commencing the date of my(our) death(s), or as soon thereafter as is practical, and continuing said distribution until:

(check one and complete where applicable)

☒ all such assets are fully distributed or paid out.

☐ ________________, 19____, on which date, the remaining balance of said Trust assets shall be paid over to said beneficiary, effectively terminating the Trust if no other assets so remain IN TRUST.

☐ said beneficiary reaches his(her) ________________ birthday, on which date, the remaining balance of said Trust assets shall be paid over to said beneficiary, effectively terminating the Trust if no other assets so remain IN TRUST.

☐ (other) ____.

Provided, however, that in the event said Beneficiary does not survive the full distribution of said assets, the balance of said undistributed assets thereby remaining shall be distributed pursuant to the beneficiary survivor provisions of Clause No. 1 of said Trust.

Whereas, under Paragraph 3(a) of said TRUST, the Trustor(s) is(are) reserved with the right to amend or modify said Trust without prior notice to or the consent of such beneficiary. Notwithstanding any other provision or provisions of said Trust that may be contrary to the manifest intents of this Amendment to said TRUST, this Amendment to said TRUST shall supercede, in all respects, all such contrary provisions, rendering the same inapplicable.

Now therefore, pursuant to such authority and right to amend said TRUST, the Trustor(s) hereby amend said TRUST by enlarging the powers of the Successor Trustee(s) to continue IN TRUST that share of the Trust assets distributable to said Trust Beneficiary FRANKLIN G. DOE, for the period and under the conditions hereinbefore designated.

IN WITNESS WHEREOF, I(we) have signed these presents this 10TH day of FEBRUARY, 19 92.

John Larsen Doe
Trustor

Sally Lois Doe
Co-Trustor

 FORM AT-601a Page 1

FORM AT-601a

AMENDMENT TO TRUST LIMITING DISTRIBUTION OF ASSETS TO A BENEFICIARY

An example of the TRUST AMENDMENT limiting a Beneficiary to monthly payments, then the balance upon receiving a College Degree.

AMENDMENT TO TRUST LIMITING DISTRIBUTION OF ASSETS TO A BENEFICIARY

KNOW ALL MEN BY THESE PRESENTS:

That I(we) JOHN LARSEN DOE AND SALLY LOIS DOE, the undersigned Trustor(s), under that certain DECLARATION OF TRUST known as (and hereafter referred to as) DOE FAMILY TRUST NO. D-1 ______,

dated FEBRUARY 1, 19 92, and pursuant to Paragraph 3(a) of said Trust, do by these presents hereby amend and modify Paragraph 11(a) of said Trust to enlarge the power of the Successor Trustee(s) to continue IN TRUST that share of the Trust assets which are determined to be distributable to Trust Beneficiary JOHN LARSEN DOE, JR. ______ and pay or disburse the same to said Beneficiary in (check one) ☒ Monthly (☐ Quarterly) (☐ Annual) payments not exceeding $ 300.00, commencing the date of my(our) death(s), or as soon thereafter as is practical, and continuing said distribution until:

(check one and complete where applicable)

☐ all such assets are fully distributed or paid out.

☐ ______, 19 ___, on which date, the remaining balance of said Trust assets shall be paid over to said beneficiary, effectively terminating the Trust if no other assets so remain IN TRUST.

☐ said beneficiary reaches his(her) ______ birthday, on which date, the remaining balance of said Trust assets shall be paid over to said beneficiary, effectively terminating the Trust if no other assets so remain IN TRUST.

☒ (other) JOHN LARSEN DOE, JR. GRADUATES FROM COLLEGE WITH A BACHELOR OF SCIENCE DEGREE IN COMPUTER SCIENCE. THE BALANCE THEN REMAINING, IF ANY, SHALL BE FULLY PAID.

Provided, however, that in the event said Beneficiary does not survive the full distribution of said assets, the balance of said undistributed assets thereby remaining shall be distributed pursuant to the beneficiary survivor provisions of Clause No. 1 of said Trust.

Whereas, under Paragraph 3(a) of said TRUST, the Trustor(s) is(are) reserved with the right to amend or modify said Trust without prior notice to or the consent of such beneficiary. Notwithstanding any other provision or provisions of said Trust that may be contrary to the manifest intents of this Amendment to said TRUST, this Amendment to said TRUST shall supercede, in all respects, all such contrary provisions, rendering the same inapplicable.

Now therefore, pursuant to such authority and right to amend said TRUST, the Trustor(s) hereby amend said TRUST by enlarging the powers of the Successor Trustee(s) to continue IN TRUST that share of the Trust assets distributable to said Trust Beneficiary ______, for the period and under the conditions hereinbefore designated.

IN WITNESS WHEREOF, I(we) have signed these presents this 10TH day of FEBRUARY, 19 92.

John Larsen Doe
Trustor

Sally Lois Doe
Co-Trustor

FORM AT-700

AFFIDAVIT OF SUCCESSOR TRUSTEE'S AUTHORITY TO ADMINISTER TRUST

An example of the AFFIDAVIT granting the Successor Trustee the authority to administer the Trust upon the death of the last Trustor.

When recorded, mail to:

Name: FRANKLIN G. DOE

Address: 456 MY STREET

City/State/Zip Code: LOS ANGELES, CA 96000

Space above this line for Recorder's use

AFFIDAVIT OF SUCCESSOR TRUSTEE'S AUTHORITY TO ADMINISTER TRUST

STATE OF ARIZONA)
) ss.
COUNTY OF PIMA)

The undersigned affiant(s) being first duly sworn on oath, deposes and says that:

I(We) am(are) the Successor Trustee(s) under that certain DECLARATION OF TRUST known as (and hereafter referred to as) DOE FAMILY TRUST NO. D-1,

dated FEBRUARY 1, 19 92, a copy of which is appended hereto and made a part hereof by reference; that NOTICE is hereby given that I(We) have assumed the duties as Successor Trustee(s) as provided under Paragraph (*check one*) ☒ 7(a) [☐ 7(b)] of said Trust; that in support of this affidavit, appended hereto is a copy of the document indicated below, to wit:

(check one)

☒ DEATH CERTIFICATE

☐ MEDICAL CERTIFICATE

That in my(our) capacity as Successor Trustee(s), all of the Trustee's rights, title and interest in and to the Real and Personal Property comprising the TRUST RES of said Trust have been assumed by affiant(s) as of this date, and that the same will be administered in accordance with the applicable provisions of said Trust.

Further affiant sayeth not.

Franklin G. Doe
Affiant-Successor Trustee

Dorothy A. Roe
Affiant-Co-Successor Trustee

SUBSCRIBED AND SWORN TO before me, a Notary Public, on this 20TH day of JANUARY, 19 98, by FRANKLIN G. DOE AND DOROTHY A ROE.

My Commission Expires: APRIIL 3, 1999

Lee C Webb
Notary Public

FORM AT-700

AFFIDAVIT OF SUCCESSOR TRUSTEE'S AUTHORITY TO ADMINISTER TRUST

An example of the AFFIDAVIT granting the Successor Trustee the authority to administer the Trust upon the medical disability of the Trustor.

When recorded, mail to:

Name: FRANKLIN G. DOE

Address: 456 MY STREET

City/State/Zip Code: LOS ANGELES, CA 96000

Space above this line for Recorder's use

AFFIDAVIT OF SUCCESSOR TRUSTEE'S AUTHORITY TO ADMINISTER TRUST

STATE OF ARIZONA)
) ss.
COUNTY OF PIMA)

The undersigned affiant(s) being first duly sworn on oath, deposes and says that:

I(We) am(are) the Successor Trustee(s) under that certain DECLARATION OF TRUST known as (and hereafter referred to as) DOE FAMILY TRUST NO. D–1 , dated FEBRUARY 1 , 19 92 , a copy of which is appended hereto and made a part hereof by reference; that NOTICE is hereby given that I(We) have assumed the duties as Successor Trustee(s) as provided under Paragraph (*check one*) ☐ 7(a) [☒ 7(b)] of said Trust; that in support of this affidavit, appended hereto is a copy of the document indicated below, to wit:

(check one)

☐ DEATH CERTIFICATE

☒ MEDICAL CERTIFICATE

That in my(our) capacity as Successor Trustee(s), all of the Trustee's rights, title and interest in and to the Real and Personal Property comprising the TRUST RES of said Trust have been assumed by affiant(s) as of this date, and that the same will be administered in accordance with the applicable provisions of said Trust.

Further affiant sayeth not.

Franklin G. Doe
Affiant-Successor Trustee

Dorothy A Roe
Affiant-Co-Successor Trustee

SUBSCRIBED AND SWORN TO before me, a Notary Public, on this 27TH day of OCTOBER , 19 97 , by FRANKLIN G. DOE AND DOROTHY A ROE .

My Commission Expires: MARCH 3, 1999

Lee C Webb
Notary Public

 FORM AT-700

FORM AT-701

MEDICAL CERTIFICATION

An example of the MEDICAL CERTIFICATION used to support the authority to the Successor Trustee to administer the Trust.

MEDICAL CERTIFICATION

Patient: JOHN LARSEN DOE

Medical Facility: EL MONTE MEDICAL CENTER

Address: 4000 W. ARCH BLVD.

City/State TUCSON, ARIZONA

Attending Physician: (NAME OF DOCTOR)

Date of this Certification: OCTOBER 27, 1997

TO WHOM IT CONCERNS:

This Medical Certification is prepared at the request of FRANKLIN G. DOE, who is, or represents himself(herself) to be, the Successor Trustee under that certain DECLARATION OF TRUST known as (and hereafter referred to as) DOE FAMILY TRUST NO. D-1 ________, dated FEBRUARY 1, 19 92, and executed by JOHN LARSEN DOE AND SALLY LOIS DOE, the Trustor or Co-Trustor under said Trust, who is a patient of the Medical Facility above-named, having been admitted as such patient on JANUARY 1, 19 94.

The undersigned, who is the attending Physician of said JOHN LARSEN DOE, hereby certifies that he(she) has conducted(or supervised) a medical examination of the said patient, and has diagnosed his(her) medical condition as follows: (DESCRIBE HERE THEACUTE MEDICAL CONDITION OF TRUSTOR)

The undersigned, in his(her) professional opinion, CERTIFIES that the nature and extent of said patient's medical(mental) condition is sufficient to cause a present impairment of his(her) normal ability to manage his(her) affairs.

FURTHER, that the undersigned disavows any liability or responsibility as to the intended application or use of this Medical Certification; and that the provisions of Clause No. 15 (Non-Liability of Third Parties) of said DECLARATION OF TRUST has full application in this instance.

IN WITNESS WHEREOF, I have signed this Medical Certification the date first above written.

(SIGNATURE OF ATTENDING DOCTOR)
Physician

ACKNOWLEDGMENT

State of ARIZONA)
) ss.
County of PIMA)

On this 27TH day of OCTOBER, 19 97, before me, the undersigned Notary Public, personally appeared, (NAME OF ATTENDING DOCTOR) ________, to me known to be the individual(s) described in and who executed the foregoing Instrument and acknowledged that he(she)(they) executed the same for the purposes therein contained.

My Commission Expires: APRIL 3, 1999

____
Notary Public

 FORM AT-701

FORM AT-702

AFFIDAVIT TERMINATING SUCCESSOR TRUSTEE'S AUTHORITY TO ADMINISTER TRUST

An example of the AFFIDAVIT terminating the Successor Trustee the authority to administer the Trust when the Trustor recovers from the medical disability.

When recorded, mail to:

Name: JOHN LARSEN DOE

Address: 123 ANY STREET

City/State/Zip Code: TUCSON, AZ 85700

Space above this line for Recorder's use

AFFIDAVIT TERMINATING SUCCESSOR TRUSTEE'S AUTHORITY TO ADMINISTER TRUST

STATE OF ARIZONA)
) ss.
COUNTY OF PIMA)

The undersigned affiant being first duly sworn on oath, deposes and says:

That I(we) JOHN LARSEN DOE ______, am(are) the Trustor(s), under that certain DECLARATION OF TRUST known as (and hereafter referred to as) DOE FAMILY TRUST NO. D-1, dated FEBRUARY 1, 19 92; that pursuant to the provisions of Paragraph 9 of said Trust, Notice is hereby given that the Trustor(s) has(have) elected to terminate the Successor Trustee's authority to actively administer said Trust under the color of authority granted to said Successor Trustee on OCTOBER 27, 19 97, in accordance with the conditions described in Paragraph 8(b), Medical Incapacity of Trustor(s), as evidenced by the AFFIDAVIT OF SUCCESSOR TRUSTEE'S AUTHORITY TO ADMINISTER TRUST, with supporting documents appended thereto; that all of the authorities, powers and rights accorded to the Successor Trustee under said Trust on OCTOBER 27, 19 97, are hereby terminated this date; and that all rights, title and interest in and to the Real and Personal Property comprising the TRUST RES shall be forthwith assigned, conveyed and transferred to me(us) as Trustee(s) under said Trust.

Further affiant sayeth not.

Dated this 1ST day of DECEMBER, 19 97.

John Larsen Doe
Trustor

______
Co-Trustor

SUBSCRIBED AND SWORN TO before me, a Notary Public, on this 1ST day of DECEMBER, 19 97, by JOHN LARSEN DOE.

My Commission Expires: MARCH 3, 1999

Lee C Webb
Notary Public

FORM AT-702

FORM AT-900

TRUST ACTIVITY RECORDING LOG

An example of the chronological record of the Living Trust activity.

TRUST ACTIVITY RECORDING LOG

Instrument	Executed by	Date	Complete, only if recorded in the Official Records				Purpose
			County/State	Date	Book/ Docket/ Volume	Page(s)	
DECLARATION OF TRUST NO. D-1 (FORMS AT-101-1 THRU AT-105	JOHN LARSEN DOE/ SALLY LOIS DOE	FEB. 1/92					ESTABLISHING THE LIVING TRUST
DEED OF REALTY TO TRUST (FORM AT-200)	JOHN LARSEN DOE/ SALLY LOIS DOE	FEB. 1/92	PIMA/ ARIZONA		9772	PG. 25-26	TRANSFER REALTY TITLE TO TRUST
QUIT CLAIM DEED TO TRUST (FORM AT-201)	JOHN LARSEN DOE/ SALLY LOIS DOE	FEB. 1/92	PIMA/ ARIZONA		6789	PG. 41-42	TRANSFER A REALTY INTEREST TO TRUST
FINANCIAL ACCOUNT TRANSFER TO TRUST (FORM AT-202)	JOHN LARSEN DOE/ SALLY LOIS DOE	FEB. 1/92					TRANSFERING BANK ACCOUNT TO TRUST
SECURITIES TRANSFER TO TRUST (FORM AT-203)	JOHN LARSEN DOE/ SALLY LOIS DOE	FEB. 1/92					TRANSFERRING STOCK TO TRUST
ASSIGNMENT OF SECURED REALTY INTEREST TO TRUST (FORM AT-204)	JOHN LARSEN DOE/ SALLY LOIS DOE	FEB. 1/92	PIMA/ ARIZONA		1134	PG. 50-51	TRANSFERING A DEED OF TRUST TO TRUST
CHATTEL TRANSFER TO TRUST (FORM AT-205)	JOHN LARSEN DOE/ SALLY LOIS DOE	FEB. 1/92	PIMA/ ARIZONA		4456	PG. 68-69	TRANSFERRING AN AUTOMOBILE TO TRUST
ASSIGNMENT OF CONTRACT TO TRUST (FORM AT-206)	JOHN LARSEN DOE	FEB. 1/92					TRANSFERRING A ROYALTY CONTRACT TO TRUST
BUSINESS INTEREST TRANSFER TO TRUST (FORM AT-207)	JOHN LARSEN DOE	FEB. 1/92					TRANSFERRING A SOLE PROPRIETORSHIP TO TRUST
THE LAST WILL AND TESTAMENT OF (FORM AT-400a-b)	JOHN LARSEN DOE	FEB. 5/92					TO MAKE A LAST WILL AND TESTAMENT

FORM AT-900

Page 1

APPENDIX B

REMOVEABLE TRUST FORMS AND PROPERTY TRANSFER INSTRUMENTS

This Appendix B includes:

FORM	DESCRIPTION
AT-101-1	Declaration of Trust, Page 1 (Each Beneficiary Equally Sharing the Trust Property)
AT-101-2	Declaration of Trust, Page 1 (Each Beneficiary receiving a Fixed Percentage of the Trust Property)
AT-101-3	Declaration of Trust, Page 1 (Each Beneficiary receiving Specific Trust Property)
AT-102-1	Declaration of Trust, Page 2 (Trust Clause No. 2, The Trust Property)
AT-102-2	Declaration of Trust, Page 2 (Trust Clause No. 2, The Trust Property with numerical listing of property)
AT-103	Declaration of Trust, Page 3 (Trust Clauses No. 3 through 8)
AT-104	Declaration of Trust, Page 4 (Trust Clauses No. 9 through 14)
AT-105	Declaration of Trust, Page 5 (Trust Clauses No. 15 through 18 and the Notary Acknowledgment)
AT-200a-b	Deed of Realty To Trust, Pages 1 and 2
AT-201a-b	Quit Claim Deed To Trust, Pages 1 and 2
AT-202	Financial Account Transfer To Trust
AT-203	Securities Transfer To Trust
AT-204a-b	Assignment of Secured Realty Contract To Trust, Pages 1 and 2
AT-205a-b	Chattel Transfer To Trust, Pages 1 and 2
AT-206	Assignment of Non-Realty Contract To Trust
AT-207a-b	Business Interest Transfer To Trust, Pages 1 and 2
AT-300	Notice of Trust
AT-400a-b	A simple Pour-Over Last Will and Testament, Pages 1 and 2
AT-500	Disclaimer by Spouse
AT-600	Amendment To Trust Enlarging Powers Of Trustee(s)
AT-601a-b	Amendment to Trust Limiting Distribution of Assets to a Beneficiary, Pages 1 and 2
AT-700	Affidavit Of Successor Trustee's Authority To Administer Trust
AT-701	Medical Certification
AT-702	Affidavit Terminating Successor Trustee's Authority To Administer Trust
AT-900	Trust Activity Recording Log

Alpha Publications of America, Inc., presents:

The all new **LIVING TRUST BINDER SET. . . .** Now you can keep your valuable Living Trust Declaration and the Trust Forms and Trust Instruments in this attractive LIVING TRUST BINDER which includes, a Grey DuPont Vinyl Matching **SLIP CASE AND 3 RING BINDER** with individualized **INDEX TABS.**

Only $17.95

With this **LIVING TRUST BINDER SET,** you can conveniently place your Living Trust Records on your Book Shelf with other books and portfolios which will provide you with easy access to your Living Trust Records.

To order your **LIVING TRUST BINDER SET,** either call our Toll Free Number 1-800-528-3494 with your Credit Card Order, or you can complete the below ORDER FORM and mail it, together with your Check or Money Order to: **Alpha Publications Of America, Inc. - 4500 E. Speedway, Suite 31, Tucson, AZ 85712.**

Cut along this line

ORDER FORM

TO:
Alpha Publications Of America, Inc.
4500 E. Speedway, Suite 31
Tucson, AZ 85712

Gentlemen:

Please send me __________ **LIVING TRUST BINDER SETS** at $17.95 each, plus Shipping and Insurance of $2.75 each set.

Name: ______________________________

Street Address: ______________________________

City/State/Zip Code ______________________________

☐ Enclosed is my ☐ Check ☐ Money Order in the amount of $__________ which includes $2.75 shipping and insurance for each Binder Set Ordered.

☐ Please charge to my Credit Card: Type: ☐ AMEX ☐ DISCOVER ☐ MASTERCARD ☐ VISA; Credit Card No. ______________________________ ; Expiration Date: __________.

____
Signature of cardholder

DECLARATION OF TRUST

(Revocable Trust)

[Trust Name (Number) ______________________________]

This DECLARATION OF TRUST made and executed this ________ day of ______________________,

19______, in the ________________ of ________________________, State of ________________,
by and between, the herein named Trustor(s) and Trustee(s):

Trustor		**Trustor**
Name: ______________________	(and)	Name: ______________________
Address: ______________________		Address: ______________________
______________________		______________________
Trustee		**Trustee**
Name: ______________________	(☐ and)(☐ or)	Name: ______________________
Address: ______________________		Address: ______________________
______________________		______________________
Successor Trustee		**Successor Trustee**
Name: ______________________	(☐ and)(☐ or)	Name: ______________________
Address: ______________________		Address: ______________________
______________________		______________________

BENEFICIARIES

Names of Beneficiaries	Percentage	Names of Beneficiaries	Percentage
______________________	______%	______________________	______%
______________________	______%	______________________	______%
______________________	______%	______________________	______%
______________________	______%	______________________	______%

WITNESSETH:

1. TRUST INTENT AND BENEFICIARY SURVIVORSHIP CLAUSE.

The Trustor(s) has(have) caused the transfer of all of his(her)(their) rights, title and interest in and to the property herein described in Clause No. 2 of this Declaration of Trust, to the above named Trustee(s) to be held In Trust for the use, benefit and enjoyment of the above named Beneficiary(Beneficiaries) who are individually designated to receive a specific and fixed percentage of the Trust Res, as indicated above under the Percentage Column; and unless otherwise hereinafter designated, said share(s) shall be (check one) ☐ the survivor(s) of them, or ☐ per stirpes, excepting for that(those) share(s) of the Trust

Property under this Trust to be distributed to Beneficiary(ies), ______________________________

____,

if he(she)(they) shall not survive me(us), shall be distributed as follows: ______________________

____.

2. TRUST PROPERTY CLAUSE.

(a) The property being initially transferred by the Trustor(s) to establish this DECLARATION OF TRUST is situated and described as follows: (Describe separately each item of property and its situate, i.e., City, County, State, etc.) ______

including any other real and/or personal property of every kind and nature which the Trustee(s) may, pursuant to any of the provisions hereof, at any time hereafter acquire, hold or cause to be made payable to this Trust, and the investments and reinvestments (all such property being hereinafter referred to collectively as the Trust Property) for the benefit, purposes and uses, and upon the terms and conditions herein set forth.

DECLARATION OF TRUST
(Revocable Trust)

[Trust Name (Number) ______________________________]

This DECLARATION OF TRUST made and executed this ________ day of ______________________,
19______, in the ______________ of ______________________, State of ______________,
by and between, the herein named Trustor(s) and Trustee(s):

Trustor		**Trustor**
Name: ______________________	(and)	Name: ______________________
Address: ______________________		Address: ______________________
______________________		______________________
Trustee		**Trustee**
Name: ______________________	(☐ and)(☐ or)	Name: ______________________
Address: ______________________		Address: ______________________
______________________		______________________
Successor Trustee		**Successor Trustee**
Name: ______________________	(☐ and)(☐ or)	Name: ______________________
Address: ______________________		Address: ______________________
______________________		______________________

BENEFICIARIES

Names of Beneficiaries	**Trust Property Number**	**Names of Beneficiaries**	**Trust Property Number**
______________________	________	______________________	________
______________________	________	______________________	________
______________________	________	______________________	________
______________________	________	______________________	________

WITNESSETH:

1. TRUST INTENT AND BENEFICIARY SURVIVORSHIP CLAUSE.

The Trustor(s) has(have) caused the transfer of all of his(her)(their) rights, title and interest in and to the property herein described in Clause No. 2 of this Declaration of Trust, to the above named Trustee(s) to be held IN TRUST for the use, benefit and enjoyment of the above named Beneficiary(Beneficiaries) who is(are) individually designated to receive certain and specific shares of TRUST RES, as indicated above under the Trust Property Number column; and unless otherwise hereinafter designated, said share(s) shall be (check one) ☐ the survivor(s) of them, or ☐ per stirpes, excepting for that(those) share(s)

of the TRUST PROPERTY under this TRUST to be distributed to Beneficiary(ies), ______________________

____,

if he(she)(they) shall not survive me(us), shall be distributed as follows: ______________________

____.

2. TRUST PROPERTY CLAUSE.

(a) The property being initially transferred by the Trustor(s) to establish this DECLARATION OF TRUST is situated and described as follows: (Describe separately each item of property and its situate, i.e., City, County and State):

Trust Property No. 1: ____________________

Trust Property No. 2: ____________________

Trust Property No. 3: ____________________

Trust Property No. 4: ____________________

including any other real and/or personal property of every kind and nature which the Trustee(s) may, pursuant to any of the provisions hereof, at any time hereafter acquire, hold or cause to be made payable to this Trust, and the investments and reinvestments (all such property being hereinafter referred to collectively as the Trust Property) for the benefit, purposes and uses, and upon the terms and conditions herein set forth.

When recorded, mail to:

Name: ______________________

Address: ______________________

____

City/State/Zip Code: ______________________

____

Space above this line for Recorder's use

DEED OF REALTY TO TRUST

(Conveying Real Property to Trust)

KNOW ALL MEN BY THESE PRESENTS:

That I(we) ______________________, the undersigned Grantor(s), who is(are) the Trustor(s) under that certain DECLARATION OF TRUST, known as (and hereafter referred to as) ______________________ ______________________, dated ______________________, 19 ______, do by these presents, hereby convey IN TRUST [(*check box if applicable*) ☐ as Trust Property No. ______] unto ______________________ ______________________, as Trustee(s) under said Trust, all of my(our) rights, title and interest in and to that certain parcel of real property situated in ______________________ County, State of ______________________, and described as: ______________________

____

____

____

____

____

The Grantor(s) asserts an interest in the aforesaid property pursuant to an instrument conveying title to real property dated ______________________, 19 ______, and recorded in the Official Land Records of ______________________ County, State of ______________________, in Docket(Book)(Volume) ______________________ at page(s) ______________________.

TO HAVE AND TO HOLD the said premises unto and to the use of the said Trustee(s) and his(her)(their) successors in interest forever; and that neither I(we) nor my(our) heirs or assigns shall have nor make any claims or demands upon said property.

IN WITNESS WHEREOF, I(we) have hereunto set my(our) hand(s) and seal this ______ day of ______ ______________________ 19 ______.

______________________	______________________
Witness (only if required under State Laws)	Grantor/Trustor
______________________	______________________
Witness (only if required under State Laws)	Co-Grantor/Co-Trustor

ACKNOWLEDGMENT(S)

State of ______________________________)
) ss.
County of ____________________________)

On this _____ day of ____________________, 19 _____, before me, the undersigned Notary Public, personally appeared ____

____,
known to me to be the individual(s) who executed the foregoing instrument and acknowledged the same to be his(her)(their) free act and deed.

My Commission Expires: ___________________ ______________________________
Notary Public

State of ______________________________)
) ss.
County of ____________________________)

On this _____ day of ____________________, 19 _____, before me, the undersigned Notary Public, personally appeared ____

____,
known to me to be the individual(s) who executed the foregoing instrument and acknowledged the same to be his(her)(their) free act and deed.

My Commission Expires: ___________________ ______________________________
Notary Public

When recorded, mail to:

Name: ______________________________

Address: ______________________________

____

City/State/Zip Code: ______________________________

____

Space above this line for Recorder's use

QUIT CLAIM DEED TO TRUST

(Releasing Real Estate Contract Interest to Trust)

KNOW ALL MEN BY THESE PRESENTS:

That I(we) ____,
the undersigned Releasor(s), who is(are) the Trustor(s) under that certain DECLARATION OF TRUST, known as (and hereafter referred to as) ____
____,
dated ____________________, 19 ______, do by these presents, hereby release, remise and forever Quit Claim IN TRUST [(*check box if applicable*) ☐ as Trust Property No. ______] unto ______________
____,
as Trustee(s) under said Trust, all of my(our) rights, title and interest in and to that certain Property situated in ____________________ County, State of ____________________,
and described as: ____
____
____
____
____
____
____

The Releasor(s) asserts an interest in the aforesaid property pursuant to an agreement(contract) to acquire said property dated ____________________, 19 ______, which said agreement(contract) is recorded in the Official Land Records of ____________________ County, State of ____________________,
in Docket(Book)(Volume) ____________________ at page(s) ____________________.

TO HAVE AND TO HOLD the said interest in the above described property unto and to the use of the said Trustee(s) and his(her)(their) successors in interest forever; and that neither I(we) nor my(our) heirs or assigns shall have nor make any claims or demands upon said property interest.

IN WITNESS WHEREOF, I(we) have hereunto set my(our) hand(s) and seal this ______ day of ______
____________________ 19 ______.

______________________________	______________________________
Witness (only if required under State Laws)	Releasor/Trustor
______________________________	______________________________
Witness (only if required under State Laws)	Co-Releasor/Co-Trustor

ACKNOWLEDGMENT(S)

State of ______________________________)
) ss.
County of ______________________________)

On this _____ day of ____________________, 19 _____, before me, the undersigned Notary Public, personally appeared ____

____,
known to me to be the individual(s) who executed the foregoing instrument and acknowledged the same to be his(her)(their) free act and deed.

My Commission Expires: ____________________ ______________________________
Notary Public

State of ______________________________)
) ss.
County of ______________________________)

On this _____ day of ____________________, 19 _____, before me, the undersigned Notary Public, personally appeared ____

____,
known to me to be the individual(s) who executed the foregoing instrument and acknowledged the same to be his(her)(their) free act and deed.

My Commission Expires: ____________________ ______________________________
Notary Public

SECURITIES TRANSFER TO TRUST

(☐ Stocks ☐ Bonds ☐ Other)

To: ______________________________

____

____

____

KNOW ALL MEN BY THESE PRESENTS:

That I (we) ____,
the undersigned Transferor(s), who is(are) the Trustor(s) under that certain DECLARATION OF TRUST, known as (and hereafter referred to as) ____

____,

dated ______________________, 19 ________, by these presents, does(do) hereby assign, transfer and deliver IN TRUST [(*check box if applicable*) ☐ as Trust Property No. ________] unto ________

____,

as Trustee(s) under said TRUST, all of my(our) rights, title and interest in and to the securities described as:

____

____

____

____

____

____

____

____;

standing in the name of the undersigned on the books of said Company.

Said Securities shall hereafter be owned by, designated and entitled on the books of said Company, as follows:

____

____.

TO HAVE AND TO HOLD the said securities unto and to the use of said Trustee and his(her)(their) successors in interest forever; and that neither I(we) nor my(our) heirs or assigns shall have nor make any claim or demand upon such securities.

IN WITNESS WHEREOF, I(we) have signed these presents this ________ day of ____________________,
19 ________.

____
Transferor/Trustor

____
Co-Transferor/Co-Trustor

PLEASE NOTE:
The signature of the Transferor(s) must be guaranteed by an officer of a commercial bank, trust company, or by a member of the New York Stock Exchange or another national securities exchange where transferor(s) has(have) an active account or signature on file. Notarized or witnessed signatures are not acceptable for securities transfers.

(Affix Signature Guaranteed Stamp Below)

FORM AT-203

When recorded, mail to:

Name: ______________________________

Address: ______________________________

____

City/State/Zip Code: ______________________________

____

Space above this line for Recorder's use

ASSIGNMENT OF SECURED REALTY INTEREST TO TRUST

(☐ Deed Of Trust ☐ Realty Mortgage)

KNOW ALL MEN BY THESE PRESENTS:

That I (we) ____,
the undersigned Assignor(s), who is(are) the Trustor(s) under that certain DECLARATION OF TRUST, known as (and hereafter referred to as) ____

____,

dated ______________________, 19______, do by these presents, hereby assign, transfer and set over IN TRUST [(*check box if applicable*) ☐ as Trust Property No. ______] unto ______________________

____,

as Trustee(s) under said Trust, all of my(our) rights, title and interest in and to that certain:

(check one)

☐ Beneficial Interest In Deed Of Trust ☐ Realty Mortgage

and to the Note or other evidence of indebtedness secured thereby, dated ______________________, 19______, and recorded in the Official Land Records of ______________________ County, State of ______________________, in Docket(Book)(Volume) ______________________, at page(s) ______________________.

TO HAVE AND TO HOLD the said Security Interest, including all benefits payable thereunder, unto and to the use of the said Trustee(s) and his(her)(their) successors in interest forever; and that neither I(we) nor my(our) heirs or assigns shall have nor make any claims or demands upon said Secured Realty Interest.

IN WITNESS WHEREOF, I(we) have hereunto set my(our) hand(s) and seal this ______ day of ______________________ 19______.

______________________________	______________________________
Witness (Only if required under State law)	Assignor/Trustor
______________________________	______________________________
Witness (Only if required under State law)	Co-Assignor/Co-Trustor

(Notary Acknowledgment On Back)

ACKNOWLEDGMENT(S)

State of ______________________)
) ss.
County of ______________________)

On this _____ day of ______________, 19 _____, before me, the undersigned Notary Public, personally appeared ______________________________

______________________________,

known to me to be the individual(s) who executed the foregoing instrument and acknowledged the same to be his(her)(their) free act and deed.

My Commission Expires: ______________ ______________________
Notary Public

State of ______________________)
) ss.
County of ______________________)

On this _____ day of ______________, 19 _____, before me, the undersigned Notary Public, personally appeared ______________________________

______________________________,

known to me to be the individual(s) who executed the foregoing instrument and acknowledged the same to be his(her)(their) free act and deed.

My Commission Expires: ______________ ______________________
Notary Public

When recorded, mail to:

Name: ______________________________

Address: ______________________________

____

City/State/Zip Code: ______________________________

____

Space above this line for Recorder's use

CHATTEL TRANSFER TO TRUST

(Transferring Personal Property to Trust)

KNOW ALL MEN BY THESE PRESENTS:

That I (we) ______________________ ______________________,
the undersigned Transferors(s), who is(are) the Trustor(s) under that certain DECLARATION OF TRUST, known as (and hereafter referred to as) ______________________
______________________,
dated ______________________, 19 ________, do by these presents, hereby assign, transfer and deliver IN TRUST [(*check box if applicable*) ☐ as Trust Property No. ________] unto ______________________
______________________,
as Trustee(s) under said Trust, all of my(our) rights, title and interest in and to the following Chattel Property, to wit: ______________________
____
____
____
____
______________________.

Said Chattel Property shall hereafter be owned by, designated and entitled, as follows: ______________________
____
______________________.

TO HAVE AND TO HOLD all of the said Chattel Property unto and to the use of the said Trustee(s) and his(her)(their) successors in interest forever; and I(we) do hereby covenant to and with the said Trustee(s) and his(her)(their) successors in interest; that I(we) am(are) the legal owner(s) of the said Chattel Property; that it is free and clear of any claims, encumbrances or liens; that I(we) have the absolute right to assign, transfer and deliver said Chattel Property as aforesaid; that I(we) am(are) in peaceable possession of said Chattel Property; and that I(we) will forever warrant and defend the same against the lawful claims and demands of all persons whomsoever.

IN WITNESS WHEREOF, I(we) have hereunto set my(our) hand(s) and seal this ______________ day of ______________________ 19 ______.

____
Transferor/Trustor

____
Co-Transferor/Co-Trustor

ACKNOWLEDGMENT(S)

State of ______________________)
) ss.
County of ______________________)

On this _____ day of ______________________, 19 _____, before me, the undersigned Notary Public, personally appeared ____

____,
known to me to be the individual(s) who executed the foregoing instrument and acknowledged the same to be his(her)(their) free act and deed.

My Commission Expires: ______________ ______________________
Notary Public

State of ______________________)
) ss.
County of ______________________)

On this _____ day of ______________________, 19 _____, before me, the undersigned Notary Public, personally appeared ____

____,
known to me to be the individual(s) who executed the foregoing instrument and acknowledged the same to be his(her)(their) free act and deed.

My Commission Expires: ______________ ______________________
Notary Public

ASSIGNMENT OF CONTRACT TO TRUST

(Non-Realty Contract)

To: ______________________________

____

____

____

KNOW ALL MEN BY THESE PRESENTS:

That I (we) ____,
the undersigned Assignor(s), who is(are) the Trustor(s) under that certain DECLARATION OF TRUST known as (and hereafter referred to as) ____

____,

dated ____________________, 19 ________, do by these Presents, hereby assign, transfer and set over IN TRUST [(*check box if applicable*) ☐ as Trust Property No. ______] unto ______________

____,

as Trustee(s) under said TRUST, all of my (our) rights, title and interest in and to that certain contract, dated ____________________, 19______, executed by ______________________________,

in favor of ____,

under the terms of which certain payments accrue to me(us) by virtue of ____________________

____

____

____

____

____.

Said Contract shall hereafter be owned by, designated and entitled, as follows: ______________

____

____.

TO HAVE AND TO HOLD the said Contract Interest unto and to the use of the said Trustee(s) and Successor(s) in interest forever, and that neither I(we) nor my(our) heirs or assigns shall have nor make any claim or demand upon such contract interest.

IN WITNESS WHEREOF, I(we) have signed these presents this ______ day of ______________, 19______.

____
Assignor/Trustor

____
Co-Assignor/Co-Trustor

State of ______________________________)
) ss.
County of ______________________________)

ACKNOWLEDGMENT

On this __________ day of ______________________, 19____, before me, the undersigned Notary Public, personally appeared, ____

____,

to me known to be the individual(s) described in and who executed the foregoing instrument and acknowledged that he(she)(they) executed the same for the purposes therein contained.

My Commission Expires: ____________________ ______________________________
Notary Public

FORM AT-206

When recorded, mail to:

Name: ______________________________

Address: ______________________________

____

City/State/Zip Code: ______________________________

____

Space above this line for Recorder's use

BUSINESS INTEREST TRANSFER TO TRUST

(☐ Sole Proprietorship ☐ Partnership)

KNOW ALL MEN BY THESE PRESENTS:

That I (we) ____,
the undersigned Transferor(s), who is(are) the Trustor(s) under that certain DECLARATION OF TRUST, known as (and hereafter referred to as) ____
____,
dated ____________________, 19________, do by these presents, hereby assign, transfer and set over IN TRUST [(*check box if applicable*) ☐ as Trust Property No. ________] unto ______________________
____,
as Trustee(s) under said Trust, all of my(our) rights, title and interest in and to that certain Business Organization known as: ____, and located at:
____, which is a (check one)
☐ Sole Proprietorship (☐ Partnership with general partners ______________________
and ______________________; my(our) interest in said partnership being ________ percent).

Said Business Interest shall be hereafter owned by, designated and entitled, as follows: ______________
____
____.

TO HAVE AND TO HOLD the said Business Interest unto and to the use of the said Trustee(s) and his(her)(their) Successors in Interest forever; and that neither I(we) nor my(our) heirs or assigns shall have nor make any claims or demands upon said Business Interest.

IN WITNESS WHEREOF, I(we) have signed these presents this ________ day of ____________________, 19________.

____
Transferor/Trustor

____
Co-Transferor/Co-Trustor

(Notary Acknowledgment On Back)

ACKNOWLEDGMENT(S)

State of ____________________)
) ss.
County of ____________________)

On this _____ day of ____________________, 19 _____, before me, the undersigned Notary Public, personally appeared ____

____,
known to me to be the individual(s) who executed the foregoing instrument and acknowledged the same to be his(her)(their) free act and deed.

My Commission Expires: ____________________ ______________________________
Notary Public

State of ____________________)
) ss.
County of ____________________)

On this _____ day of ____________________, 19 _____, before me, the undersigned Notary Public, personally appeared ____

____,
known to me to be the individual(s) who executed the foregoing instrument and acknowledged the same to be his(her)(their) free act and deed.

My Commission Expires: ____________________ ______________________________
Notary Public

THE LAST WILL AND TESTAMENT
of

____

I, ______________________________ ,
also known as ______________________________ ,
a resident of the ______________ of ______________ ,
which I do declare to be my place of domicile, being of sound and disposing mind and memory, do hereby make, publish and declare this to be my Last Will and Testament, thus revoking all Wills and Codicils to Wills previously made by me.

FIRST (Debt Clause): I direct that the Executor(Executrix) hereinafter named pursuant to this Last Will and Testament, pay (as soon after my death as practical) all of my just debts and obligations, including funeral expenses and the expenses incident to my last illness, but excepting those long term debts secured by real or personal property which may be assumed by the person designated to receive such property.

SECOND (Distribution Clause): I give, devise and bequeath all of the rest, remainder and residue of my estate, whether real or personal property of whatsoever kind or character, and wherever situated, to the Successor Trustee named and appointed by me under that certain Declaration Of Trust, known as ______________________________
______________________________ , dated ______________ , 19 ______ ,
as then written or thereafter amended, to be added to the property then held IN TRUST and become one and a part of the Trust Corpus, subject to the terms and conditions of said Declaration Of Trust, except the following property, if any, which shall be given as follows:

____
____
____
____
____
______________________________ .

THIRD (Common Disaster Clause): If my spouse, if any, shall die as a result of a common disaster with me, then my spouse shall be deemed to have (check one): ☐ survived me (☐ predeceased me).

FOURTH (Survivorship Clause): If any person(s) named in this Last Will and Testament, other than my spouse, shall not survive me, then that share of my estate which would have been distributed to such person(s) had he(she)(they) survived me, shall be distributed (*check one*): ☐ per stirpes (☐ per capita).

FIFTH (Executor(Executrix) Appointment Clause): I hereby nominate, constitute and appoint as the Executor (Executrix) of my Estate: ______________________________ ,
provided, however, that in the event he(she) is unable or unwilling to so serve in such capacity, then I nominate, constitute and appoint ______________________________ .

SIXTH (Guardian Appointment Clause): I hereby nominate, constitute and appoint as the Guardian of any minor child(ren) of mine: ______________________________ ,
provided, however, that in the event he(she) is unable or unwilling to so serve in that capacity, then I nominate, constitute and appoint ______________________________ .

SEVENTH (Saving Clause): In the event any separate provision of this Last Will and Testament is held to be invalid by a Court of competent jurisdiction, then such finding shall not invalidate this entire Last Will and Testament, but only the subject provision.

IN WITNESS WHEREOF, I have hereunto signed this, my Last Will and Testament, this ______ day of ______________ , 19 ______ , in the ______________ of ______________ ,
State of ______________ .

____
Testator(Testatrix)

ATTESTATION CLAUSE

The foregoing Last Will and Testament was on the above date, subscribed, sealed, published and declared by the Testator(Testatrix), above named, as his(her) Last Will and Testament in the presence of each of us below named Witnesses, and at the same time, we at his(her) request in his(her) presence and in the presence of each other who hereunto subscribed our names as witnesses hereto; this Attestation Clause having been first read aloud and we hereby certify that at the time of the execution hereof, we believe the Testator(Testatrix) to be of sound and disposing mind and memory.

______________________________ of ______________________________
Address

____
City State

______________________________ of ______________________________
Address

____
City State

______________________________ of ______________________________
Address

____
City State

AFFIDAVIT TO SELF-PROVE LAST WILL AND TESTAMENT[1]

State of ______________________)
) ss.
County of ______________________)

WE, ______________________, ______________________,

and ______________________, the witnesses whose names are signed to the attached or foregoing instrument, being first duly sworn, do hereby declare to the undersigned authority that the testator(testatrix) signed and executed the foregoing instrument as his(her) Last Will and Testament, that he(she) had signed willingly (or willingly directed another to sign for him(her), that he(she) executed it as his(her) free and voluntary act for the purposes therein expressed; that each of the witnesses, in the presence of each other and hearing of the testator(testatrix), signed the Last Will and Testament as witnesses; and that to the best of their knowledge, the testator(testatrix) was at that time eighteen years of age or older, of sound mind and under no constraint or undue influence.

____
Witness Signature

____
Witness Signature

____
Witness Signature

SUBSCRIBED AND SWORN to before me this ________ day of ______________________, 19 _____.

My Commission expires: ______________________ ______________________
Notary Public

Note 1. This Affidavit merely self-proves the Last Will and Testament in the event all of the Witnesses are unavailable when this Will is probated. It is not, therefore, required to validate this Will, but only an option (see Note 2.).

Note 2. This Last Will and Testament is a witnessed Will which means it will not be valid unless it is witnessed (signed) by the number of witnesses required under State Laws who do not have an interest in the estate of the person making this Last Will and Testament. (*See: Witness Requirements,* Page 11 of Instruction Guide)

When recorded, mail to:

Name: ______________________________

Address: ____________ ______________

____

City/State/Zip Code: ______________________

____

Space above this line for Recorder's use

DISCLAIMER BY SPOUSE

This DISCLAIMER BY SPOUSE, executed this ______ day of ________________, 19 ____, by ______________________________, the undersigned (check one) ☐Husband (☐ Wife) of ______________________________, hereinafter referred to as the "spouse";

Whereas:

1. The spouse is the Trustor under that certain DECLARATION OF TRUST known as (and hereafter referred to as) ______________________________ ______________________________, dated ________________, 19 ____;

2. The spouse has heretofore acquired certain property either with his(her) separate funds or by gift or bequest; said property being situated in ______________ County, State of ______________, and described as: ______________________________ ______________________________ ______________________________.

3. The undersigned has no past or present claim, interest. lien, rights or title in and to the above described property;

4. The undersigned waives all community property rights, curtesy or dower rights and/or any other rights to said property which may be accorded to me under applicable State Laws, if any.

NOW THEREFORE, in consideration of the premises, the undersigned does hereby disclaim, remise, release and quit claim unto the aforesaid Spouse, his(her) heirs and assignees forever, all rights, title, interest, claim or demands which the undersigned might have, or appear to have under law, in and to the above described property.

IN WITNESS WHEREOF, I have signed this DISCLAIMER BY SPOUSE, the year and date first above written.

____
Witness(only if required under State Laws)

____
Signature of Disclaiming Spouse

____
Witness(only if required under State Laws)

ACKNOWLEDGMENT

State of ______________________)
) ss.
County of ______________________)

On this __________ day of ______________________, 19 ____, before me, the undersigned Notary Public, personally appeared, ______________________________, to me known to be the individual described in and who executed the foregoing Instrument and acknowledged that he(she) executed the same for the purposes therein contained.

My Commission Expires: ______________

____
Notary Public

FORM AT-500

AMENDMENT TO TRUST
ENLARGING POWERS OF TRUSTEE(S)

To: ____

____

____

____

KNOW ALL MEN BY THESE PRESENTS:

That I(we) ____,
the undersigned Trustor(s) under that certain DECLARATION OF TRUST known as (and hereafter referred to as)
____
____,
dated ______________________, 19 ______; and pursuant to the applicable provisions of said TRUST, do by these presents, hereby amend said TRUST to clarify, define, enlarge, modify, or otherwise grant to Trustee(s) unrestricted authority and power under Paragraph 6(a) of said TRUST, to ______________________________________
____
____
____
____
____
____

WHEREAS, under Paragraph 3(a) of said TRUST, the Trustor(s) has(have) the authority, right and power to amend or modify said Trust.

NOW THEREFORE, pursuant to such authority, right and power to amend said TRUST, the Trustor(s) hereby elect to amend Paragraph 6(a), Powers of the Trustee(s), to include those powers herein described.

IN WITNESS WHEREOF, I(we) have signed these presents this __________ day of ______________________,
19 ________.

____
Trustor

____
Co-Trustor

ACKNOWLEDGMENT

State of ________________________________)
) ss.
County of ______________________________)

On this ________ day of ________________________, 19 ______, before me, the undersigned Notary Public, personally appeared, ____
____,
to me known to be the individual(s) described in and who executed the foregoing Instrument and acknowledged that he(she)(they) executed the same for the purposes therein contained.

My Commission Expires: ________________________ ________________________________
Notary Public

FORM AT-600

AMENDMENT TO TRUST LIMITING DISTRIBUTION OF ASSETS TO A BENEFICIARY

KNOW ALL MEN BY THESE PRESENTS:

That I(we) ______________________________,
the undersigned Trustor(s), under that certain DECLARATION OF TRUST known as (and hereafter referred to as) ______________________________
______________________________,

dated ______________, 19____, and pursuant to Paragraph 3(a) of said Trust, do by these presents hereby amend and modify Paragraph 10(a) of said Trust to enlarge the power of the Successor Trustee(s) to continue IN TRUST that share of the Trust assets which are determined to be distributable to Trust Beneficiary ______________________________ and pay or disburse the same to said Beneficiary in (check one) ☐ Monthly (☐ Quarterly) (☐ Annual) payments not exceeding $______________, commencing the date of my(our) death(s), or as soon thereafter as is practical, and continuing said distribution until:

(check one and complete where applicable)

☐ all such assets are fully distributed or paid out.

☐ ______________, 19____, on which date, the remaining balance of said Trust assets shall be paid over to said beneficiary, effectively terminating the Trust if no other assets so remain IN TRUST.

☐ said beneficiary reaches his(her) ______________ birthday, on which date, the remaining balance of said Trust assets shall be paid over to said beneficiary, effectively terminating the Trust if no other assets so remain IN TRUST.

☐ (other) ______________________________
____
____
____
____
______________________________.

Provided, however, that in the event said Beneficiary does not survive the full distribution of said assets, the balance of said undistributed assets thereby remaining shall be distributed pursuant to the beneficiary survivor provisions of Clause No. 1 of said Trust.

Whereas, under Paragraph 3(a) of said TRUST, the Trustor(s) is(are) reserved with the right to amend or modify said Trust without prior notice to or the consent of such beneficiary. Notwithstanding any other provision or provisions of said Trust that may be contrary to the manifest intents of this Amendment to said TRUST, this Amendment to said TRUST shall supercede, in all respects, all such contrary provisions, rendering the same inapplicable.

Now therefore, pursuant to such authority and right to amend said TRUST, the Trustor(s) hereby amend said TRUST by enlarging the powers of the Successor Trustee(s) to continue IN TRUST that share of the Trust assets distributable to said Trust Beneficiary ______________________________, for the period and under the conditions hereinbefore designated.

IN WITNESS WHEREOF, I(we) have signed these presents this ________ day of ______________,
19______.

____
Trustor

____
Co-Trustor

ACKNOWLEDGMENT

State of ________________________________)
) ss.
County of ________________________________)

On this ______ day of __________________________, 19______, before me, the undersigned Notary Public, personally appeared ____

____,

known to me to be the individual(s) who executed the foregoing instrument and acknowledged the same to be his(her)(their) free act and deed.

My Commission Expires: ______________________________ ____
Notary Public

When recorded, mail to:

Name: ______________________________

Address: ______________________________

____

City/State/Zip Code: ______________________________

____

Space above this line for Recorder's use

AFFIDAVIT OF SUCCESSOR TRUSTEE'S AUTHORITY TO ADMINISTER TRUST

STATE OF ______________________________)
) ss.
COUNTY OF ______________________________)

The undersigned affiant(s) being first duly sworn on oath, deposes and says that:

I(We) am(are) the Successor Trustee(s) under that certain DECLARATION OF TRUST known as (and hereafter referred to as) ______________________________
______________________________,
dated ______________________________, 19 ______, a copy of which is appended hereto and made a part hereof by reference; that NOTICE is hereby given that I(We) have assumed the duties as Successor Trustee(s) as provided under Paragraph (*check one*) ☐ 7(a) [☐ 7(b)] of said Trust; that in support of this affidavit, appended hereto is a copy of the document indicated below, to wit:

(check one)

☐ DEATH CERTIFICATE

☐ MEDICAL CERTIFICATE

That in my(our) capacity as Successor Trustee(s), all of the Trustee's rights, title and interest in and to the Real and Personal Property comprising the TRUST RES of said Trust have been assumed by affiant(s) as of this date, and that the same will be administered in accordance with the applicable provisions of said Trust.

Further affiant sayeth not.

____
Affiant-Successor Trustee

____
Affiant-Co-Successor Trustee

SUBSCRIBED AND SWORN TO before me, a Notary Public, on this ______ day of ______________,
19 ______, by ______________________________.

My Commission Expires: ______________________________

____
Notary Public

FORM AT-700

MEDICAL CERTIFICATION

Patient: ______________________________

Medical Facility: ______________________________

Address: ______________________________

City/State ______________________________

Attending Physician: ______________________________

Date of this Certification: ______________________________

TO WHOM IT CONCERNS:

This Medical Certification is prepared at the request of ______________________________, who is, or represents himself(herself) to be, the Successor Trustee under that certain DECLARATION OF TRUST known as (and hereafter referred to as) ______________________________

______________________________,

dated ______________, 19____, and executed by ______________________________

______________________________, the Trustor or Co-Trustor under said Trust, who is a patient of the Medical Facility above-named, having been admitted as such patient on ______________________________, 19____.

The undersigned, who is the attending Physician of said ______________________________, hereby certifies that he(she) has conducted(or supervised) a medical examination of the said patient, and has diagnosed his(her) medical condition as follows: ______________________________

____

____

____

____

____

The undersigned, in his(her) professional opinion, CERTIFIES that the nature and extent of said patient's medical(mental) condition is sufficient to cause a present impairment of his(her) normal ability to manage his(her) affairs.

FURTHER, that the undersigned disavows any liability or responsibility as to the intended application or use of this Medical Certification; and that the provisions of Clause No. 14 (Non-Liability of Third Parties) of said DECLARATION OF TRUST has full application in this instance.

IN WITNESS WHEREOF, I have signed this Medical Certification the date first above written.

____

Signature of Attending Physician

ACKNOWLEDGMENT

State of ______________________________)

) ss.

County of ______________________________)

On this ________ day of ______________________________, 19____, before me, the undersigned Notary Public, personally appeared, ______________________________

______________________________,

to me known to be the individual(s) described in and who executed the foregoing Instrument and acknowledged that he(she)(they) executed the same for the purposes therein contained.

My Commission Expires: ______________ ______________________________

Notary Public

When recorded, mail to:

Name: ______________________________

Address: ______________________________

____

City/State/Zip Code: ______________________________

____

Space above this line for Recorder's use

AFFIDAVIT TERMINATING SUCCESSOR TRUSTEE'S AUTHORITY TO ADMINISTER TRUST

STATE OF ______________________________)
) ss.
COUNTY OF ______________________________)

The undersigned affiant being first duly sworn on oath, deposes and says:

That I(we) ______________________________ ______________________________, am(are) the Trustor(s), under that certain DECLARATION OF TRUST known as (and hereafter referred to as) ______________________________ ______________________________, dated ______________________________, 19______; that pursuant to the provisions of Paragraph 8 of said Trust, Notice is hereby given that the Trustor(s) has(have) elected to terminate the Successor Trustee's authority to actively administer said Trust under the color of authority granted to said Successor Trustee on ______________________________, 19______, in accordance with the conditions described in Paragraph 7(b), Medical Incapacity of Trustor(s), as evidenced by the AFFIDAVIT OF SUCCESSOR TRUSTEE'S AUTHORITY TO ADMINISTER TRUST, with supporting documents appended thereto; that all of the authorities, powers and rights accorded to the Successor Trustee under said Trust on ______________________________, 19______, are hereby terminated this date; and that all rights, title and interest in and to the Real and Personal Property comprising the TRUST RES shall be forthwith assigned, conveyed and transferred to me(us) as Trustee(s) under said Trust.

Further affiant sayeth not.

Dated this ________ day of ______________________________, 19______.

____
Trustor

____
Co-Trustor

SUBSCRIBED AND SWORN TO before me, a Notary Public, on this ________ day of ______________________________, 19______, by ______________________________.

My Commission Expires: ______________________________

____
Notary Public

FORM AT-702